small spaces

small spaces

TERENCE CONRAN

conran
OCTOPUS

To my Grandchildren. To help them enjoy small spaces.
Sam, Max, Felix, Coco, Finbar, Rose and Harry, and Tom and Cynthia's
who is enjoying a very small space as I write this.

First published in 2001 by
Conran Octopus Limited
a part of Octopus Publishing Group
2–4 Heron Quays, London E14 4JP
www.conran-octopus.co.uk

Publishing Director: Lorraine Dickey
Commissioning Editor: Bridget Hopkinson

Consultant editor: Liz Wilhide

Creative Director: Leslie Harrington
Design: Lucy Gowans
Location and picture research: Clare Limpus
Special photography: Thomas Stewart
Styling for special photography: Lyndsay Milne

Production Director: Zoë Fawcett
Production: Alex Wiltshire

British Library Cataloguing-in-Publication Data.
A catalogue record for this book is available from the British Library.

ISBN 1 84091 161 1

Printed in China

contents

introduction

Space is the greatest luxury of our time

In urban areas, where more and more of us live today, this is particularly true: one has only to glance at the property pages, or skim over the details displayed in estate agents' windows, to appreciate the increasing premium placed on what might once have been considered only average accommodation. Factor a desirable location into the equation and 'average' shrinks to downright tiny.

Opposite: New York architects LOT/EK, who specialize in creative recycling, sited an old truck container on the roof of a Manhattan housing block to add an extra room to an existing apartment. This rough-edged 'penthouse' has had walls and roof removed at one end to provide an outdoor terrace.

If space is expensive in cities, it is also in cities where our need for it is most acute. Metropolitan life is life in a crowd – packed commuter trains, traffic-clogged streets and busy offices mean that many of us spend our working days with a shortage of both physical and mental elbow room. It is one thing to repair to a snug cottage after a bracing walk on a windswept moor,

Above left: Small by anyone's standard, but with a certain elemental appeal, the organic structure of the igloo provides shelter at its most basic.

Above right: Award-winning, eco-friendly and portable, this Swedish-designed holiday retreat redefines the mobile home.

quite another to battle one's way through the rush hour only to feel the pinch at home. Given the pace and pressure of urban living, it is no wonder that most of us think of spatial quality in terms of quantity alone.

Dream houses are almost never small; real houses – and flats – often are. Whether or not they live in cities, most people find themselves at some stage or another in the unavoidable position of cutting their dreams down to size, and putting up with rather less than they had originally intended. But living areas that are limited in scale do not have to be lacking in other respects. The purpose of this book is to show how to create space by intelligent design and to demonstrate that small is not always a compromise; that small, indeed, can be beautiful.

Any discussion of small spaces begs the question, what exactly is small? Like many spatial concepts, the notion of 'smallness' is somewhat relative. One-room living is by its nature generally on the small side – unless you are talking about a true industrial-scaled loft, rather than a bedsit. A two-bedroom

apartment may be a squeeze for a family of four, but remarkably commodious for a single person. But there is more to the issue than the sheer amount of square metres per person. A house may superficially appear to provide generous accommodation, but be laid out in such a way that some areas are too cramped to function well. Then, again, circumstances do change and a home that is perfectly adequate as a domestic base may feel too constrained if you decide to make it your work place as well. Human nature being what it is, most of us would probably like to live somewhere just that little bit bigger – which means that you do not need to be camped in a broom cupboard or rabbit hutch to benefit from the ideas and solutions explored in these pages.

Above left: Small spaces, such as this boathouse festooned with lanterns, need not be lacking in appeal.

Above right: A room with a view: the quirky charm of a lifeguard hut, South Beach, Miami, USA.

Below left: Nowhere in the world is space at such a premium as Japan. Pod-like enclosures make minimal overnight accommodation at this Tokyo hotel – definitely not for the claustrophobic!

The first step in thinking 'small' is to think positive. The high market value of space has a tendency to reinforce the view that a small area is necessarily substandard, second-best. This, in turn, tends to obscure the many advantages, both practical and psychological, that small spaces can offer.

Practically speaking, small spaces are generally more cost-effective to run and maintain in terms of heating, lighting and cleaning. Large period houses, for example, date from the days when there was a ready supply of domestic labour, an army of servants who toiled away behind the scenes keeping everything ticking over. Even with modern appliances and technology, running such a household today can be very demanding in terms of time and effort, particularly if both partners are in full-time employment. Then again, large

Above: Space-saving is all about flexibility. This Australian bed on runners offers the choice between sleeping indoors or, weather permitting, under the stars.

Opposite: The NhEW House is an eco-friendly structure made of lightweight modular panels assembled on a hinged aluminium frame. Designed to be portable, adaptable and to fit like a second skin, it can be insulated for cold weather.

spaces do not necessarily remain spacious for very long. There is a sort of unwritten domestic law whereby clutter will tend to expand to fill the space available, whatever its size – a version of 'nature abhors a vacuum', perhaps. In this respect, small spaces can ultimately be less wasteful as they place a physical full stop to mindless accumulation.

In terms of psychological advantages, chief among the emotional benefits of a small space must be the feeling of cosiness. The recent fad for minimalism might seem to indicate that cosiness is no longer rated very highly on the contemporary domestic wish-list. But it takes a particular type of person to find vast amounts of empty space ultimately comfortable; the instinct to create a sense of enclosure – a nest – is rooted deep in the human psyche. For our ancestors, caves, camps and fortified buildings provided both shelter from the elements and protection from invaders, but just as domesticated animals such as cats and dogs are innately programmed to seek out small, confined

spaces even when their surroundings pose no real threat, the same sense of security remains important for people, too.

There is a difference, however, between cosiness and claustrophobia. Psychologists have explored the close relationship between agoraphobia and claustrophobia; such apparently opposite fears can, in fact, be suffered by the same person. In the same way, a space that exposes and isolates can be as uneasy in its effect as one that is excessively confining. A large, open space can make you feel small, which is not a very agreeable feeling at all. Cosiness, on the other hand, implies a quality of ease and rightness, of a space that is scaled to human needs and limitations.

In *The Poetics of Space*, French philosopher Gaston Bachelard sees the house as a place that enshrines 'memories of protection'. But it is also a place, according to Bachelard, that allows our more specific memories of different times and events to be contained or 'housed'. He goes on to say that 'if the house is a bit elaborate, if it has a cellar and a garret, nooks and corridors, our memories have refuges that are all the more clearly delineated'. Such retreats 'have all the value of a shell'. This feeling of intimacy, or protection, or cosiness, explains much of the irresistible appeal of small spaces such as window seats, alcoves and inglenooks.

Many similar places are no less delightful for being limited in scale. In this context, it is worth spending some time thinking about spaces you have experienced that have aroused such feelings. I remember once staying in a hotel in Stockholm where the rooms were incredibly tiny. Being a largeish person – not the ideal build, perhaps, for a small space – I was slightly horrified when I was first shown my room. After only a short while,

Above: A former lighthouse on the coast of Maine, USA, makes a snug retreat away from it all. Quality of space is not necessarily a function of size: small is often delightful.

Above right: A box bed tucked into an alcove has all

the cosiness of a ship's cabin, with plenty of storage available in the pull-out drawers beneath. The neatness and hard-working nature of such fitted spaces is all part of the appeal.

however, I realized that I felt amazingly relaxed. Whoever had designed the room must have had all the ingenuity of a boat-builder, as everything was so compact and neatly fitted out. A television set mounted on the ceiling lowered to a viewing position at the touch of a button; a little table could be swung out from a wall; there was even a wooden seat in the shower that flapped down to provide a temporary perch. Set in an alcove and screened by a shutter, there was a bureau with writing materials laid out on top; a light came on when you lifted the shutter to make a cosy working area. You did require something of a tutorial to understand how it all worked – a training manual would have been helpful – but the intricate functionality of the space was a true pleasure.

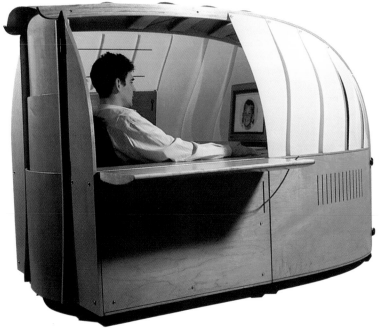

I suspect that the attraction of that Stockholm hotel room had a great deal to do with the sense that one was in total command of one's surroundings – that, in effect, the room could be 'driven' like a car, with all the controls within easy reach. A few years ago, at the Design Museum in London, I noticed that the same type of response was provoked by a self-contained work space, which was one of the designs on show in a Conran Collection exhibition. Created by Douglas Ball, the Clipper CS-1 work station consisted of a pod-like structure with blinds, creating a private enclosure where concentrated work could be undertaken without distractions. The shape of the pod was friendly and organic, the materials – plywood and canvas – were natural and sympathetic, but the real draw of the design was its obvious associations with a cockpit. Absolutely everyone wanted to sit in it.

Transport provides many points of reference for small space design. Life on the open road holds a particular attraction if you take your home with you. Before he succumbed to the glamour

Below: Like the flight deck of a jet, good small space design gives you the sense of being in control.

of the motorcar in *The Wind in the Willows*, Toad's first passion was for a little 'canary-coloured cart', a gypsy caravan fitted out with everything anyone could possible want. 'It was indeed very compact and comfortable. Little sleeping-bunks – a little table that folded up against the wall – a cooking stove, lockers, bookshelves, a bird-cage with a bird in it; and pots, pans, jugs and kettles of every size and variety.' Toad, no doubt, would have been similarly beguiled by the sleek, streamlined contours of an Airstream trailer or one of the meticulously fitted out canal boats that provide floating homes in cities such as London and Amsterdam. Many years ago, I travelled through India in a railway carriage that provided accommodation for seven of us, together with a number of servants. The carriage had its own kitchen and was parked in sidings at night; in its functional detailing and appearance it rather resembled the sleeper train in the film *Some Like It Hot*. Sleeping on trains offers a very special sort of comfort and our compact travelling 'hotel' contributed enormously to the excitement of the journey.

Such examples serve as powerful reminders of the intrinsic appeal of small spaces. But, like the cottage on the windswept moor, charm often depends to a large extent on context. Small hotel rooms make sympathetic, functional bases simply because one isn't stuck in them most of the time; while the cosy caravan or railway carriage serves as a secure refuge when one is constantly on the move, experiencing new places. Although many of the features evident in such designs can be successfully adopted at home, what is more often required are the types of spatial strategies that generate a sense of expansiveness.

Marc Newson's recent design for Ford, the 021C, is a striking example of how to create a sense of space in a confined area. Although the 021C is actually smaller than a Ford Ka, Newson has achieved a remarkable feeling of spaciousness by turning certain standard concepts of car design on their heads. Instead of a central door pillar between front and rear doors, the front door is hinged at the front and the rear door is hinged at the rear, so that they open rather like French windows, providing

clear, unobstructed access to the interior. Inside, similarly, the gear box is set into the floor pan so there is no central column to divide the floorspace, a feature that also allows the front seat to be an uninterrupted bench. Exterior details spell out the same sense of clarity, simplification and economy – both front and rear headlamps are in the form of continuous strips, rather than individual lights. The design reminds me of an old Citroën traction avant that I used to own, which had both bench seats and a flat floor – not a very large car, but one that also felt spacious inside, rather like a small sitting room with the windscreen as your television.

Lack of obstruction, clear access and simplicity of detailing – the strategies employed by Newson in the design of his car – can equally be applied to the problem of small interior spaces, and in the first chapters of the book similar architectural solutions, which make the most of available space, are explored. Allied to these fundamental design issues is the importance of making sympathetic decorative choices – schemes that maximize light and provide vitality and interest without serving to close in the walls.

Above: Marc Newson's concept design for Ford, the O21C, achieves a great feeling of space.

Opposite from top: Life on the move provides plenty of inspiration for small space living. This elegant 1940s mobile living van was made by Vosper (top). The classic Brayshaw is a showman's wagon dating from the early twentieth century (centre, top). Barges provide compact living with a unique sense of style; this Amsterdam barge comes with a working fireplace and parquet flooring (centre and below).

Above: The Airstream trailer, with its sleek, streamlined contours, is a classic of the open road.

But the way in which a home is designed and decorated is only half the story when it comes to creating a sense of spaciousness. The other half is what you put into it. Good home organization is more than shoe tidies and shelving, it involves a fairly radical reappraisal of all our belongings and the manner in which they are used and stored. For many people, myself included, it's a rather thorny problem, particularly as it goes to the heart of why we acquire things and, more importantly, why we continue to hang on to them. The fact that we are fortunate to have this problem at all, that by and large we enjoy such a degree of affluence that getting rid of things is more of an issue than getting hold of them in the first place, in no way takes the sting out of the situation.

If, as Bachelard says, homes house memories, some of the memories they house come in the tangible forms of objects, items of clothing, chairs, tables, pictures, books... When you live in a small space, you will arrive at the point sooner rather than later when some serious evalution of your possessions must take place. After all, one of the best ways of gaining more cupboard space is to put less in your cupboards.

Although today we increasingly have to live in smaller spaces out of necessity, it is a trend that at least accords with the fluidity of modern lifestyles and which is ameliorated to a large extent by techology. Victorian and Edwardian houses were laid out in such a way as to keep the sexes, classes and generations apart: servants in the attics and 'below stairs', children in nurseries and schoolrooms, men and women each with their different domains. The extent of the segregation is evident in the fact that many large houses in town or country featured separate staircases, so that servants could scuttle about their duties unseen. Today, such a hierarchical disposition of space is both unpalatable and faintly ridiculous.

At the same time, in the days before washing machines and vacuum cleaners, dishwashers and refrigerators, cleaning and maintaining houses not only required plenty of staff, it also demanded plenty of space where the tools and utensils required to complete such tasks the long way round could be housed. 'Below stairs' often consisted of a warren of small rooms, each devoted to a specific activity. While it is doubtful that any house ever existed where the butler had his own special room for ironing the morning copy of *The Times*, such profligacy with space is by no means unknown, even today – one of the rooms in the mansion belonging to multimillionaire American producers, the Spellings, is reportedly set aside solely for the purpose of wrapping presents.

After the Second World War in Britain, when social barriers began to come down, few of those who had left domestic service to go into the forces or take up war work were prepared to go back into it. For the first time many middle class wives found themselves in the position of having to look after their families with no outside assistance. In many cases, the fairly comfortably off gave up their large households in favour of smaller homes or flats that could be managed by one person. Then, as women increasingly sought paid work outside the home, the need for spatial efficiency became ever more acute.

Today, the formality and compartmentalization of Victorian life are well and truly gone. What has also changed is the very nature of the household itself. Over the last 30 years in Britain, the number of households made up of a single person or a child-free couple has doubled and now stands at over 60 per cent of the national total. In urban areas, that percentage is greater. This

Above: Holiday homes, with their easy informality and blurring of boundaries between indoors and out, are useful reminders of the advantages of keeping living spaces simple.

astonishing demographical change, the result of late child-rearing, divorce and other social factors, has redefined the nature of the home. In place of many individual rooms, each with its own prescribed use and pattern of occupancy, has come the free, flexible, multipurpose space that accommodates different activities and the demands of different household members, including those, such as stepchildren, who may not live permanently in one place all of the time.

The French architect Le Corbusier famously stated that 'the house is a machine for living in', a phrase that traditionalists have

Above and left: The tree house is one of the most evocative of small spaces. This example in Ayrshire, Scotland, provides an arboreal dining hall, fully fitted with lighting, hot and cold water, and a range.

often gleefully seized upon as proof of the soullessness at the heart of modern design. Nothing could have been further from Le Corbusier's intentions. The quotation comes from his seminal work, *Towards a New Architecture*, published in 1923, a book that has since acquired the status of a modernist manifesto. The house is a 'machine' in the sense that its purpose or function is to facilitate living. Le Corbusier contrasts this ideal with the old nineteenth-century disposition of space: 'The existing plan of the dwelling-house takes no account of man and is conceived as a furniture store… It kills the spirit of the family, of the home…'

And, at the end of a long list of recommendations, he advises: 'Take a flat which is one size smaller than what your parents accustomed you to. Bear in mind economy in your actions, your household management and in your thoughts.'

Design on a small scale provides the opportunity to create a balance between the need for enclosure and the need for breathing space. It also encourages us to take a long hard look at our possessions, so that things we acquire or choose to keep are those that will stay the course, do the job or enhance our lives in other, more emotional ways. Most importantly, perhaps, the best small spaces represent not so much a way of surviving on the bare minimum, but a refinement, a distillation of what really matters and what really works.

This page and opposite:
An empty turret on top of a
Manhattan apartment
building has been converted
into a library on two levels,
providing a private retreat
with an unbeatable panorama
of Central Park.
Below left: On the Kerala
coast in India a traditional
betelwood and bamboo boat
makes a serene floating
hotel for travellers in search
of tranquillity.

conceptual spaces

In many ways good small space design
means adopting a new mindset.

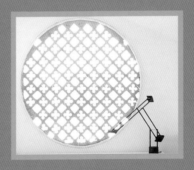

Right: A mezzanine level provides additional floor area without compromising the sense of volume within a space or blocking light and views. Here, a platform bathing area within a double-height bedroom takes the notion of the 'en-suite' bathroom a step further.

In many ways, good small space design means adopting a new mindset. Although the same basic principles apply whatever the size and scale of your home, there is a much greater need to consider design issues holistically when space is tight. The more limited the space, the greater the chance that whatever changes you implement will have a knock-on effect, which is why it is important to avoid tackling problems in a piecemeal fashion.

All design is the art of the possible. To achieve an efficient use of the space you have available, or to create new space, you first need to assess how you actually live and build up a detailed picture of your present and future requirements. At the same time, you need to acquire a thorough understanding of structure and servicing – how buildings work and what spatial changes are both physically possible and legally permissable. The best solutions arise only when both sides of the issue are properly explored and digested.

It is also important not to assume that just because space is limited there is only one way of making it work for you. A variety of options may well achieve similar results and a key part of the process is to evaluate them all, so that you end up with the one that promises greatest flexibility. The hardest-working and most efficiently designed small space will not only accommodate your needs now, but will also provide room for change at some point in the future.

Opposite: Neat detailing and consistency of surfaces and finishes are key factors in good small space design. Here, a compact kitchen on a mezzanine level serves an adjacent dining area. The reinforced glass worktop provides minimal disruption of views through the space. Fridge and freezer are concealed behind cupboards at the head of the stairs.

Time and money also come into it. Any significant spatial change requires plenty of both – resources you may prefer to spend in different ways. Before you embark on a major project, make sure that you will at least recoup your investment and that you are prepared to put up with the disruption.

ASSESSING YOUR NEEDS

Historical precedent, together with the way most property is marketed, encourages us to think of space in terms of rooms with specific functions: bedrooms, dining rooms, living rooms, and so on. This mental blueprint, in turn, has a tendency to influence our shopping list of requirements when it comes to spatial design. At the same time, much housing, both old and new, conforms to certain patterns; sheer familiarity with the way space is conventionally laid out and apportioned can stand in the way of our ability to conceive more creative and lateral solutions.

The first step in making an assessment of your needs is to wipe the slate clean of such preconceptions. Forget about rooms and their notional uses and focus instead on how you actually live and the activities that you need to accommodate within a space or series of spaces. This exercise in assessment forms the basis of your design brief.

GENERAL REQUIREMENTS

Begin by identifying your current priorities, and think about how your life may change in the near future.

● Which possessions do you intend to keep at all costs? Many belongings will fit into any space provided you organize them properly, but others – a cherished piano or an antique armoire, for example – are more demanding in terms of space.

● Which amenities are important to you? Access to outdoor areas? Plenty of kitchen storage? A separate working area?

● In which area of life do your belongings naturally tend to accumulate? Do you have a space-consuming hobby or interest?

● How long do you anticipate living in your home? If you are thinking about moving sooner rather than later, cosmetic improvements may be a better bet than saddling yourself with the expense and disruption of major spatial changes.

● How much money can you realistically afford to spend improving your home? Can you face the inevitable disruption?

● Which changes can you envisage happening to your family life, current circumstances, or pattern of employment?

COOKING

The notion of the kitchen as the heart of the home is so ingrained that it is easy to forget that only a couple of centuries ago many people lived without much in the way of cooking facilities, and depended on cookshops to roast their meat and bake their pies. Today, the wheel has come full circle and some service flats for single professionals have been designed with only the most rudimentary kitchen areas or in some cases no kitchens at all.

How much space you require for a kitchen obviously depends on the type of cook you are, how often you cook and for whom. I say obviously, but it is evident that wish-fulfillment sometimes plays too strong a role in this department. Kitchens have become status symbols of interior design and many of the most lavishly appointed and spacious examples belong to wannabe cooks rather than to those who are actually preparing meals on a regular basis. If you enjoy cooking, experiment

with new recipes, like to entertain or have a family to feed, you will need to apportion more of your available space to cooking than if you are simply keeping yourself refuelled between social engagements and realistically need no more than a microwave and a kettle. You should also take into account your pattern of shopping, since a great deal of kitchen area is often occupied by food storage. A small kitchen makes sense if you shop little and often, but you will need more space if you bulk-buy or prefer to stock up in quantity at longer intervals.

With proper extraction systems and perhaps an element of screening, cooking is one activity that can usefully be integrated with other areas, such as eating and general living spaces. Furthermore, a small space need be no real handicap when it comes to kitchen efficiency. The most ergonomic kitchen layouts tend to be fairly compressed, with the main points of activity – the hob, oven, fridge, sink and preparation zones –

no more than a few paces apart so that routine tasks can be performed without too much trotting to and fro. Incorporating the kitchen within a larger, multipurpose area means that there is the opportunity to maintain a sense of connection with the rest of the household. Even if the actual working area is tightly planned, you will feel much less confined if there are views through to other spaces, rather than solid enclosing walls.

EATING

It is fair to say that the separate dining room is an endangered species today, threatened both by lack of space and a sea-change in eating habits. A room that lies empty for most of the day represents something of an indulgence for most households; but gone, too, is the formality of dining and much of the attendant paraphernalia, both of which demanded this sort of setting. Most people who still have dining rooms seem to have turned them into home offices these days.

Left: A metal worksurface, breakfast bar and serving counter in one extends the kitchen to an outdoor eating area in a contemporary version of the old serving hatch idea.

Opposite top: If there is sufficient head height, a mezzanine level can provide much-needed space for an extra bedroom, with room beneath to take clothes storage. Toplighting in the form of skylights or rooflights helps to counter any sense of excessive enclosure.

Opposite bottom: There's something quite appealing about sleeping under the eaves, provided there is enough room to get in and out of bed comfortably. Attic conversions often work particularly well as bedrooms, offering an extra degree of privacy away from the main run of the household.

Eating, as a social activity, lends itself to a location which is not shut off from the mainstream, but is incorporated either within the main living space or in close proximity to the kitchen – or both. The bonus of this type of arrangement is that an eating area can double up as a useful focus for other activities between meals. The simple spatial equation rests on how many people in the household regularly sit down together to share a meal, which will obviously determine the size of table and number of chairs. If you like to entertain from time to time, larger gatherings can be accommodated in a variety of different ways, none of which requires a permanent, space-consuming solution.

In single-person households where space is very tight, eating areas can effectively be shrunk to a countertop, breakfast bar or flap-down table, with folding chairs and a table held in reserve for the occasions when guests come to supper.

SLEEPING

Sleeping and small spaces naturally go together. As long as your bed is big enough and comfortable enough, the cosiness of a small space can provide a welcome sense of security and privacy. In this context, high-level spaces on mezzanine levels can be very effective as sleeping platforms and require only minimal separation from other living areas – but, beware, making a bed properly on a mezzanine can be pretty difficult.

The problem arises not so much with actual sleeping arrangements, but with all the other functions that are conventionally associated with bedrooms, chief among which is the storage of clothes. Hopping in and out of bed requires a certain margin of free space – enough for easy access and easy bed-making – but dressing and undressing, storing clothes, shoes, accessories and cosmetics requires rather more. Keeping your entire wardrobe in your bedroom, particularly if you do not have much room at your disposal, can undermine its prime function as a place of peaceful retreat.

One obvious answer is to accommodate clothes storage within an adjacent hallway or other connecting space. Separate dressing areas allow you to restrict furnishings in the bedroom to a minimum and hence make do with a smaller space. A wall of built-in cupboards and shelves, tailor-made to the size and contents of your wardrobe, often represents a better use of the available area than attempting to fit the same amount of storage into a room that is already dominated by a large piece of furniture.

Family life means that you may need to review sleeping arrangements at several key intervals. Families and small spaces are not necessarily incompatible, but children do place extra demands on what is already a fairly exacting brief. Small babies may be happy sleeping in a cot in the corner of your room, but relatively quickly you will need to provide them with a space of their own and it makes good practical sense if that space is as big as possible. Many people make the mistake of assuming that simply because children are small, they require less room than adults, forgetting that many of the things that children need and want to do require plenty

of space – and that if these activities cannot be accommodated in their own room, they will take place absolutely everywhere else.

A child's bed may be a place of refuge at nighttime, but by day it is simply a springboard to action. When children are small, it is often best to allocate them as much space as possible so that their room can serve as a playroom, homework area and indoor sports arena combined, easing pressure elsewhere in the home. By the time they have reached their teenage years, their needs will have changed again and much smaller spaces can be perfectly adequate, provided each child has their own room.

Far left: Variations on the mezzanine-level bedroom theme display the versatility of the basic idea. A free-standing structure incorporates a securely anchored ladder and space for storage and study underneath.

Left: Platform sleeping areas are just as appealing as bunkbeds as far as children are concerned. Transparent panels fixed to guardrails beside the beds maintain visual lightness while providing an extra degree of safety; an en-suite bathroom is slotted in below.

Below left: A staircase provides access to this snug sleeping space – definitely not an arrangement for those prone to rolling out of bed!

Right: Awkward sloping angles and restricted head height can sometimes limit useful floor area in attic conversions. Here a bathroom layout has been planned to gain maximum use of space, with the foot of the tub extending into the eaves.

BATHING

If space is severely limited, it is a safe bet that what is conventionally termed 'the smallest room' is going to stay that way. Ideas for juggling the layout of bathroom fixtures and fittings in a confined area are covered in subsequent sections, but at this planning stage a certain degree of lateral thinking can come in useful. Unlike kitchens, where tight planning can be an aid to efficiency, very small bathrooms can bring different functions into uncomfortable proximity. One solution is to separate the lavatory from the

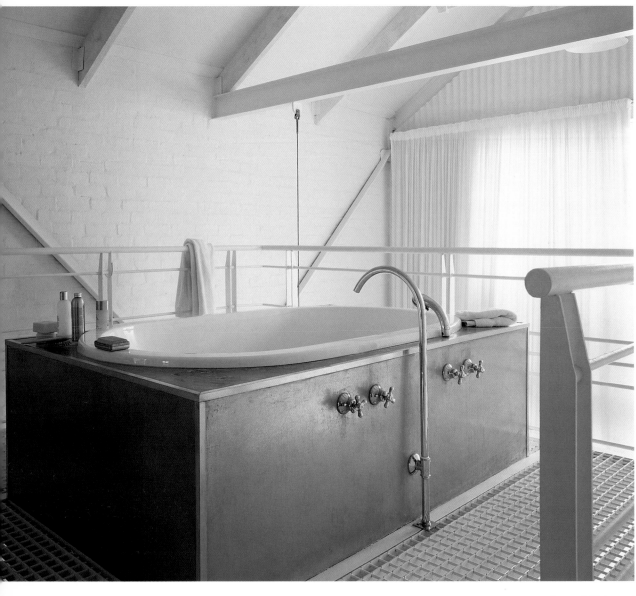

Left and below: Bathing and sleeping areas make good spatial partners. This mezzanine-level bedroom incorporates a generous free-standing bathtub set into a steel-grating platform which is suspended from the ceiling beams. A sense of spaciousness is achieved with only a minimal loss of privacy.

bathing or washing area, an arrangement that can also ease congestion at key periods of the day. If there is not enough room for even this element of segregation you could treat the entire bathroom as a wet room, with a shower draining directly into the floor. It is worth bearing in mind that a generous shower will always be more satisfactory than a cramped tub. Remember that existing drainage layouts may impose certain limitations on your plans.

Right: Flooring that is raised up a couple of steps marks the boundary between the relaxing and eating ends of the room. Pull-out drawers incorporated within the raised portion of floor provide additional storage space.

RELAXING

Living areas often lack a settled definition, not least because they increasingly serve as multipurpose spaces accommodating a wide range of different activities. Yet their most important role, and one which increases in significance the smaller your home, is to serve as a breathing space.

People choose to relax in a variety of ways but enjoying one's free time often means having some free space in which to unwind. In confined surroundings, where most areas are hard-working and tightly planned, the place that you set aside for relaxation should be as uncluttered as possible to provide an oasis of calm and redress the balance.

Even when floor area is limited, a feeling of spaciousness can be achieved by creating new openings to outside areas, by toplighting or by removing a portion of the ceiling to double the volume. Such design strategies make use of views and vistas to counteract a sense of enclosure.

Above: If your work is largely desk-bound, it may be readily accommodated within a bedroom. This simple work space, essentially no more than a broad shelf or worktop for a monitor and keyboard, makes an unobtrusive addition to a sleeping area.

Above: When assessing spatial potential, don't overlook the between-spaces of hallways and landings. This reasonably generous and well-lit landing provides optimum conditions for a compact study corner.

Left: A bay window provides a natural site for a bedroom work space. A particular advantage of this arrangement is the view; it is easier to concentrate if you can literally turn your back on the rest of the room.

Opposite: A working area on a mezzanine offers a degree of separation in a multipurpose space.

WORKING

Working from home is an increasing trend, but one that places an extra burden on small space design. How you integrate your working life with your home life will depend to a large extent on the nature of your work and how permanent an arrangement is required.

Desk-bound jobs that require little more than a dedicated thinking space and somewhere to plug in the laptop are the easiest to accommodate, provided there is some degree of separation from other areas of the home. Choosing the right location is half the battle. Depending on preference, a work station can be slotted into a corner of a sleeping area, kitchen or living room, whichever spot maximizes efficiency and minimizes disruption. Work that requires specialist equipment or extensive storage may entail the conversion of redundant areas such as basements or attics.

ASSESSING YOUR SPACE

Once you have identified your particular needs
and the type of activities for which you must
cater, the other side of the issue is to make an
assessment of the space at your disposal. A
scale drawing or even a sketch plan can be a real
asset in this preliminary process – measure areas
as accurately as possible and note principal
features, such as doors, windows, built-in
cupboards, fireplaces and other architectural
details. Getting it down on paper helps to bring

matters into focus and reveal what would
otherwise not be apparent when you are
wandering around from room to room
daydreaming about possibilities.

● Note the orientation of each area. The quality of
light has a profound effect on the way we
perceive space. Which rooms receive morning
light? Which rooms are sunny in the afternoon?
Which areas receive little natural light at all?

● Consider the flow of air. Good ventilation (not
drafts) is essential in small spaces.

Above and opposite:

A skilful blend of old and new
sites a bedroom on a
mezzanine level under an
existing beamed ceiling. A
simple staircase provides
secure access, neatly
detailed to include cupboard
space and bookshelves.

Opposite: The serene and contemplative quality of the traditional Japanese interior is an obvious point of reference for this minimally detailed sleeping space.

● Establish if there are any under-used areas. Hallways, landings and under-stairs spaces can be remarkably generous in older properties, while basements and attics may be ripe for conversion.

● Which areas are particularly cramped?

● Are there any significant architectural details that you wish to retain?

● Look at the pattern of circulation, the way in which you move from area to area. If there is more than one door to a room, which entrance do you rarely use?

● Can any improvements be made to external access?

UNDERSTANDING STRUCTURE

Many types of spatial change, not merely the most ambitious, require the expert assistance of an architect, designer, surveyor or friendly builder. Even so, it is a good idea to acquaint yourself with how the basic structure of your home works – if only to ground your plans in reality. Tales abound of over-enthusiastic home-improvers who knocked down one wall too many, only to find their home collapsing around their ears. Understanding structure is a necessary precaution against such potential disasters, but will also help to set parameters to your scheme.

Most houses, no matter what their size or of what materials they are constructed, conform to a similar pattern. Structurally speaking, the key elements are the foundations, external walls, floors, some (but not all) internal walls and the roof. The entire weight of the house rests on the foundations, which anchor the structure to the ground and give it stability. External walls bear the weight of the floors that span between them, along with the weight of the roof. Some internal walls also serve to support the floors. The roof acts

to brace the whole structure and give it rigidity.

In larger buildings, such as old commercial premises or industrial warehouses, the structural systems may be rather more complex. Where external walls are widely spaced apart, the roof may be supported by internal columns or large tie-beams or trusses. The situation is different again in the case of modern concrete- or steel-framed multistorey buildings, where little, if any, of the internal elements generally play a role in supporting the structure, and walls, both inside and out, serve as mere partitions or infills.

On the domestic scale, however, the principal issue is determining which internal walls are structural or semi-structural and which are not. In older houses, one of the simplest ways of finding out which walls are structural is to examine the direction of the floorboards. Floors are generally supported by timber joists or beams, which typically run from the front of the house to the rear. Floorboards are laid on top of the joists and at right angles to them, which means that they are usually laid across the width of the house. The internal walls that help carry the joists will be structural, and these are likely to be the walls that run across the width of the house. Other semi-structural walls are those positioned directly beneath walls at upper levels. The remaining internal walls are likely to be mere partitions, which means that they have no structural role to play.

Rapping on the wall is another popular way of distinguishing between a wall that is structural and one that is a partition – partition walls, made of studwork, will sound hollow in comparision to structural walls which are generally solid masonry. This method, however, is not infallible. In older houses, you may get a hollow sound from a

structural wall where the plaster has become 'blown' or detached in places. You may also find that a stud wall is supporting the floor above.

Changes that affect any of the main structural elements – external walls, floors, roof, foundations, internal load-bearing walls – will necessarily affect the way the house is supported. If you remove part of a structural element you weaken the entire system, and some compensating factor will be required. Take away a big chunk of a structural wall, for example, and you will need to install a beam above the new opening to carry the load. Other types of structural change may require that the foundations are strengthened or that joists are doubled up. An architect, engineer or surveyor will be able to calculate proposed changes to existing loads and specify the correct form of compensation.

Some forms of structural alteration are obvious; others less so. The following procedures generally have structural implications and will require expert assistance:

- Making new openings in external walls, such as installing a window, door or French windows, in order to connect with outside areas or with a new extension.
- Enlarging existing openings in external walls. Widening windows or a doorway to make French windows are structural procedures; increasing the size of an opening by removing the lower portion of wall – for example, turning a window into a doorway – may not necessarily be structural.
- Making new openings in load-bearing internal walls or removing them altogether.
- Removing chimney breasts. Alterations to chimney breasts, which are generally located either on party or external walls, may entail

repairs to structural walls and replacing parts of floors. Such changes may also affect ventilation.

- Resiting a staircase. Alterations to stairs inevitably entail changes to floors.
- Removing sections of floor to open out a space from level to level.
- Excavating basements below the level of the foundations.
- Converting an attic into a habitable room. The ceiling joists at the uppermost level are rarely strong enough to bear the weight of furniture and people and will probably need to be strengthened or doubled up.
- Removing a portion of the roof to create a dormer window. A dormer, which is a projecting structure, imposes an extra load on a building. A rooflight, which is merely cut from the plane of the roof, has no such structural implications.
- Adding a new storey on top of your house or on top of an existing extension.

CHANGES TO SERVICING & INFRASTRUCTURE

Servicing – gas, electricity, heating, water, drainage and communication – are your home's lines of supply and can also be a limiting factor when it comes to alteration. Many spatial changes will necessarily involve changes to services as well; in fact, such alterations can be the most disruptive and expensive part of the whole process. In nearly all cases, work must be carried out by qualified professionals or the relevant utility. At the same time, extensive renovation and redesign or the creation of new areas provide an opportunity to review your home's servicing arrangements and possibly build in some space-saving features.

- If you need to make changes to your electrical

supply, take the opportunity to provide more power points, especially in kitchen or living areas. The more sockets you have, the greater the flexibility of room use – which is a positive asset in a tightly planned space.

● Rewiring can also provide an excuse to update lines of communication by networking computers, installing ISDN lines or installing programmable lighting and music systems.

● Drainage is usually arranged in a vertical stack or a core. When planning spatial changes, either group bathrooms, utility and kitchen areas centrally or, in the case of a storeyed house, site them one above the other.

● Slimline or low-level radiators permit more flexible furniture arrangement and consume less space. Although expensive, underfloor heating or convection heaters sunk in trenches are even less intrusive. Vertical radiators can be a good idea in tiny bathrooms and kitchens where available wall space is limited.

● Ensure that all cabling and pipework is routed through walls and concealed from view. Servicing should be as discreet as possible to avoid visual disruption that can compromise the quality of space. Nothing undermines a sense of space more than a disorganized tangle of wires, conduits and pipes.

● In multipurpose areas or in a confined space, good ventilation is essential. All windows and rooflights should open fully to draw in fresh air. Invest in good extract systems for kitchens and bathrooms; by law, those that lack windows must have an extract system installed.

● Open-plan areas can be noisy, particularly if there are uncarpeted floors and a minimum of soft furnishings. Acoustic insulation within the floor will help to minimize sound travelling to the level below; wall and ceililng insulation may be required to prevent sound levels rising too dramatically within a space.

● Structural changes may also provide the opportunity to upgrade heat insulation. If you are partitioning a space, make sure that both new areas have their own radiators.

LEGALITIES

As if expense, disruption, dust and no-show builders are not enough to be getting on with, many types of spatial change require official inspection and approval by the relevant authorities. As with any other branch of the law, ignorance is no defence and if you unwittingly set about to change your home in a way that does not conform to health and safety, fire or building regulations or that is in breach of local planning laws, you may find yourself having to undo what you have done or put it right at your own cost. These regulations vary from country to country and area to area; they are also often subject to change. For these reasons, it is essential to get expert, informed advice at the beginning of any major building project. In the case of a really large or ambitious scheme, you may wish to retain the services of an architect who can oversee the progress of the work right the way through and deal with the bureaucratic issues at the correct stages. He or she may also help you to challenge some of the more absurd planning requirements.

PLANNING PERMISSION

Major changes that affect the external appearance of your home or add substantially to its floor area or volume are likely to require planning permission. Before the first builder has so much as drunk his first cup of tea, your outline proposals must be

Above: Non-domestic properties offer great potential for conversion and often have a strong architectural character of their own, as demonstrated by this vaulted cellar. Permission for change of use is increasingly welcome, especially in urban areas.

submitted to the local planners for consideration and public consultation. Neighbours have the right to object to your plans and may be successful in blocking them, particularly if they can prove that the effect of your proposals would be a loss of natural light in their own property. Even if your home is not in a conservation area, planners may insist that your scheme is designed in such a way as to blend in with the character and conform to the height of surrounding properties.

Planning permission is generally required:
● If you are splitting your home into two separate dwellings.
● If you are changing the shape of your roof.
● If you are installing a dormer window that looks out over the side or front of the house.
● If you are adding on an extra storey, either to the top of your house or to the top of an existing extension.
● If you are extending your home at ground level beyond a specified distance, over a specific height or in such a way as to increase the 'cubic content' of your home by more than 10 per cent.
● If you are building onto party walls shared with neighbours.
● If you propose to convert a building or portion of a building from industrial or commercial use into residential accommodation. Increasingly, many authorities welcome 'change of use', particularly as a means of regenerating run-down urban areas; in other areas, however, permission may be more difficult to obtain.
● The most stringent restrictions of all concern alterations to historic buildings or those situated within a conservation area. In Britain, very few changes are permitted to either the exteriors or interiors of houses listed Grade I; in the case of those listed Grade II, there is more scope for internal

alteration, provided that elevations remain the same. It may be necessary to contact heritage groups for advice on permitted materials, finishes and architectural details.

OTHER REGULATIONS

Planning permission is not the only official hurdle to overcome. Any changes to your home that involve structural alterations will need to be approved by a building inspector, whether or not planning permission is required. Then there are regulations concerning health and safety, drainage and protection from fire, which may have an impact on a wide range of design issues, from size and siting of windows and doors, to detailing of staircases and choice of construction materials.

Strictly speaking, any work that is carried out must comply with such regulations in order to be legal. Minor infringements of the building code are not unknown, however, infringements that architects or their clients consider aesthetically important – witness the number of 'illegal' staircases lacking handrails featured in architectural and interiors magazines. It is far from uncommon practice for details that a designer considers to be inelegant to appear just long enough to gain the necessary official approval, then vanish overnight. This is not to advocate such a course of action. By and large, building regulations are designed for your own safety and for the protection of your property and the properties of your neighbours. It should be perfectly possible for a design to be elegant and legal at the same time.

It is important to bear in mind the following building requirements:

● All 'habitable' rooms must have at least one window. In this context, kitchens, bathrooms and

Above: One of the easiest ways of gaining more space is to convert an attic into a habitable room. The minimum requirement is to provide some form of daylighting: a new window or rooflight, for example.

Opposite: Open plan arrangement of cooking, eating and living areas creates a seamless flow of activities and does not detract from the robust architectural character of this loft apartment, with its original exposed beams and sloping roof.

circulation spaces such as hallways and landings are not considered habitable rooms.

- New drains will need to be inspected and approved before the work is covered up.
- Soil stacks have to be extended away from new windows.
- Power points must be installed a certain distance above the floor, not flush with it, to prevent the risk of water coming into contact with the electrical supply.
- Staircases must have handrails.
- Fire regulations are particularly stringent. Stairways in houses over three storeys must be 'protected', which means that there must be some form of separation between the stair and the spaces it connects to in order to allow safe escape in case of fire.
- Don't be discouraged by bureaucracy. Although at times during the course of construction you may wish you had never started, it will be worth it in the end.

CREATING A SENSE OF SPACE

Just as we are accustomed to thinking about our homes as collections of different rooms, each with a defined function, we also tend to equate space simply with floor area. Thinking about space solely in terms of square metres, however, is to ignore a critical issue, which is the illusory quality of space.

Volume is a key consideration. To take an obvious example, rooms that are the same width and length, but which differ in height, will feel quite dissimilar. Changes to levels, such as removing portions of an upper floor to open out a space vertically, may not win you enough spare centimetres to squeeze in a big sofa – in fact it will effectively result in a loss of floor area – but

may still serve to create a sense of spaciousness, which can be the next best thing.

In a similar way, one of the most popular contemporary means of creating a feeling of space is to remove internal partitions. Again, such changes rarely result in a direct increase in floor area, but what they do achieve is the expansiveness that derives from enhanced views and vistas. If you consider the typical terraced house pattern, for example, opening up from front to rear will result in a double-aspected space, with natural light coming from two directions to the benefit of all areas within it. When the front to rear axis can be continued to include views through to outdoor areas, that sense of expansiveness is vastly increased.

Creating a single large space from several small enclosed areas permits the freedom and fluidity that is a hallmark of modern lifestyles, an inclusiveness that, oddly enough, was first expressed over a century ago by William Morris. 'The house that would please me,' he wrote, 'would be some great room where one talked to one's friends in one corner, and ate in another and slept in another and worked in another.'

It is hard to better such a summary of what one might call today the 'loft' ideal. But Morris was, perhaps, not so much anticipating future developments as harking back to the medieval past, when most households occupied precisely that sort of multipurpose space and the relentless division of home and work that came about with the Industrial Revolution had not even been envisaged.

Yet if Morris's comment implicitly celebrates living without the conventional barriers of walls, the inherent disadvantages of such an arrangement are also plain. It can be difficult to

'talk to one's friends in one corner' if the television is blaring in another; hard to concentrate on work while the preparations for dinner are in full swing a metre away. When a single space must accommodate every activity, clashes are bound to occur and there may be times when you long to retreat to a room, no matter how small, and close the door behind you.

In a similar way, much space in older houses is often devoted to corridors, hallways, landings and staircases. Removing the walls that separate halls from living areas and opening out stairwells can dramatically increase the sense of space, but at the sacrifice of what traditionally have served as mediating zones between public and private areas, or between inside and outside.

There is something essentially democratic and unpretentious about one-space living and there is little doubt that a single large area is infinitely more exhilarating and theatrical than a series of small rooms. But, at the same time, open space can be noisy, distracting and

psychologically wearying. Even when you have very little space to play with, some privacy is still important. Enclosed areas provide both a physical and emotional counterpoint, an opportunity to change gear. They also serve to highlight the contrast with open-plan areas, a shift of sensibility that enriches spatial experience.

The answer is to strive for some type of balance between openness and enclosure. This does not necessarily entail a return to traditional patterns of layout, with a number of distinct rooms connected by circulation space. Rather, it can be more liberating to consider flexible areas that can be partitioned and enclosed within a space as a whole as and when the need arises. At the end of the day, it is your decision to make, in accordance with how you want to live.

PROPORTION & CHARACTER

When you are making spatial changes within an existing structure it is important to consider the finer points of architectural character.

In older properties, for example, if you remove a wall that separates two rooms, you may find you have created a space that has two fireplaces and two chimney breasts lined up along the length of one wall. Unless you wish to go to the considerable structural trouble of removing one of the fireplaces and chimney breasts, a solution to the visual oddity might be to retain a portion of dividing wall to either side of the new opening, so that a suggestion of the old layout remains. Another remedy is to introduce a slight change of level, so that one end of the space is raised up a step or two. This can also serve the purpose of defining different zones within a multipurpose space. Similarly, when you open up a space by removing a portion of floor, you may

Left: This tiny apartment, only 36 square metres in total, is tightly planned to make maximum use of available space. While the bedroom and living areas are interconnected to preserve the quality of light, the kitchen retains its own doorway to keep cooking smells to a minimum.
Opposite: Storage space under this high-level bed is screened with a simple curtain. An extensive use of white and natural neutrals generates a feeling of spaciousness and tranquillity.

reveal windows that are inappropriately scaled: small windows will look faintly ridiculous when the space they light is much larger.

Dividing space can bring equivalent problems. Creating an enclosed area – such as a new bathroom or study – by partitioning off a portion of a larger room often means that the new space has too high a ceiling for its floor area. Lowering the ceiling to adjust the proportions will make a more visually comfortable result.

A conversion of an existing building – whether it is a humble Victorian terrace or a structure that once had an industrial, commercial or institutional use – brings to light issues concerning architectural detailing. In the bad old days, 'modernizing' generally meant ripping out historical features such as decorative mouldings, panelling and fireplaces. Not long after, the pendulum swung in the opposite direction and architectural salvage yards did a roaring trade supplying period features to home-owners bent on sympathetic restoration. Original details provide buildings with character and flavour, but at the same time, an excess of detailing can undermine a sense of spaciousness. Conversion should entail considering which features and details contribute positively to the final design and developing a sympathetic blend of old and new.

MAKING NEW SPACE

Reconfiguring an existing layout may provide you with better spatial quality, more natural light, better views and improved access, but if you physically need more space, you will either have to convert otherwise redundant areas or extend your home outwards or upwards. Such changes tend to be more expensive and complicated and almost all require professional advice.

One of the most straightforward ways of gaining extra floor area is to add another level within an existing space. This, of course, means having a space that is high enough in the first place to accommodate such an insertion. Mezzanine levels are a common feature of lofts and converted warehouses, for the very good reason that they maintain the open quality of a large space while providing somewhere to get away from it all. Essentially platforms, they make good sleeping or working areas, offering an element of privacy and separation from main living spaces. Access can be as basic as a ladder and there is no legal requirement in terms of head height – if you are happy sleeping within only a metre of the ceiling there's nothing to stop you. It has to be said, however, that mezzanines work best in what might be called true lofts, rather than the type of pseudo loft that is little more than an apartment carved out of a non-domestic building. Real lofts generally have such high ceilings that the addition of a mezzanine will create a proper space where you can actually stand up, along with room-sized accommodation underneath, which can usefully provide space for a bathroom, storage or study. This type of alteration does not require planning permission, but you will need advice from an architect or surveyor on the structural implications, since you will be increasing the load carried by the main walls.

Another relatively simple way of gaining more space is to convert an existing attic. In many older properties attic space can be quite extensive and may be virtually unused. In newer houses, however, this type of conversion is often impossible due to the use of preformed trusses in the structure of the roof. Structurally speaking, converting an attic generally entails strengthening the ceiling joists to support the weight of people and furniture, a procedure that involves doubling up the joists by adding extra beams that run alongside. Another requirement is to add at least one opening in the roof – a single rooflight that lies in the plane of the roof is the minimum. Rafters on either side of the rooflight might also require strengthening. If there is not sufficient head height, you will need to construct a dormer, which will bring other structural issues into play and requires planning permission to boot.

The other key issue is how you access the new space. If converting an attic transforms your home into a three- or four-storey dwelling, various fire regulations come into play. You may need to install a fire door to separate the new area from the rest of the house and a simple folding ladder may be unacceptable as a means of escape. In any case, if you intend to use the new space on a regular basis – and there is little point in undertaking the conversion if you do not – a proper staircase will add immeasurably to your ease and convenience.

Attic or loft conversions are deservedly popular, particularly in heavily built-up areas. The same is not true of basement conversions, which are not only infinitely less appealing, but are also much more complex and costly to execute. If your home has a proper cellar that offers enough head height, the principal work required, apart from damp-proofing and installing servicing, is to excavate the ground outside in order to install some form of external opening. On the other hand, if the basement space is shallow, the structural implications are almost prohibitive as you would need to underpin existing foundations in order to dig down further, a procedure that is as disruptive as it is expensive.

Extending the boundaries of your home, rather than converting spaces within it, is a major exercise, but one that can make all the difference between a home that is liveable and one that is not. One of the most common home extensions is the conservatory or part-glazed garden room which forms a transitional living area between indoors and out. Small conservatories do not require planning permission; a wide range of different styles are marketed in kit form and require only a little foundation work and competent assembly. For more complicated projects you will almost certainly need the services of an architect who will be able to advise on siting and the manner in which the extension relates to existing areas.

Extensions do not need to be large to be highly effective. A small matter of a metre or so on the width or length of a space can make all the difference when it comes to layout; many extensions also offer the opportunity to introduce toplighting in the form of skylights or glazed roofs, which can dramatically alter the way you experience your home as a whole. Adding an extension to your home provides an ideal opportunity for reconfiguring existing internal spaces, setting up new vistas, and improving the relationship between indoors and out.

In structural terms, ground-level extensions will require proper foundations, which may have to be tied in to existing ones. Extensions over roofs may mean that existing foundations have to be strengthened. Adding on to your home will involve making some type of opening in an external wall to form the connection between the new space and the old and, obviously, the new area will also require services in the form of electricity, drainage and heating.

case study
LONDON STUDIO FLAT

Located on the top floor of one of the blocks that comprise the Golden Lane Estate in the City of London, this tiny studio flat benefits from a vaulted ceiling and large expanses of glazing that bring natural light flooding in from both sides. At only 30 square metres, however, space is extremely limited.

When the present owner, an architect, bought the flat, the bedroom was screened off by a dividing wall that compromised the sense of space. Rather than rush into matters, however, she decided to live with the existing arrangement for a while to assess how the space worked, and to determine exactly what she needed. Her eventual solution was to open up the flat as much as possible by removing the partition wall and creating an elevated platform for the bed, with ingenious tailor-made storage underneath. Spending time thinking about how best to plan the space paid dividends. Removing the dividing wall not only maximized the sense of space, it improved access to the kitchen.

Decorative decisions emphasize the new spatial quality. Fussy detailing and carpets were removed, walls were painted white with a hint of purple for warmth, and buff-coloured linoleum was laid throughout the studio to provide a seamless neutral background. Furnishings have deliberately been kept to a minimum and every conceivable space has been used for storage. The result makes the most of the flat's strong architectural character and light, airy qualities.

Above: Open walkway at the top of one of the blocks on the listed Golden Lane Estate, designed in the 1950s by Chamberlain Powell Bon.

Opposite: Access to the platform bed is provided by a mobile stair that incorporates seven storage cubbyholes in the spaces between the treads. The stair unit is light enough to be moved about if necessary.

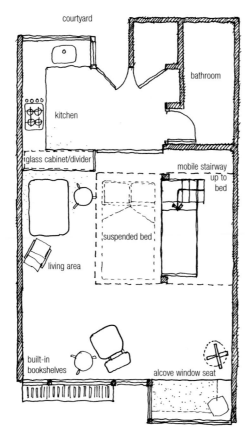

LONDON STUDIO FLAT 30 square metres

Above left: The sleeping platform, designed with the help of a structural engineer, comprises white-painted steel rafters bolted to one wall and cantilevered out into the space so that it appears to float over the floor.

Above: Once the original dividing wall was removed, access to the kitchen could be improved. A narrow doorway was replaced by a sliding panel which screens the kitchen from view when required. The glass-backed cabinet was an original built-in feature; mahogany veneer was added to match the wooden window frames.

Opposite: The platform bed makes use of the extra head height offered by the vaulted ceiling. There is even storage in the bedhead.

Left: Detail of the built-in kitchen cabinet which forms a transparent barrier between kitchen and living space.

Below left: Additional storage space is provided under the cushions of the window seat. The bookcase is an original feature.

Above: The existing kitchen and bathroom were left relatively unchanged. Additional storage on the right was created by copying the existing kitchen cabinets and a stainless steel worktop was fitted to tie it all together. The wall between the kitchen and the bathroom includes storage space for cleaning materials hidden behind touch-release panels.

Opposite: The desk unit tucked under the platform is constructed from MDF and perforated hardboard. On the other side, it incorporates a wardrobe.

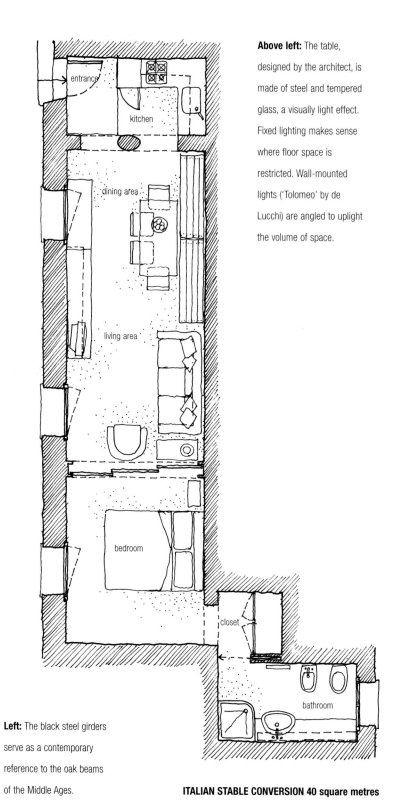

Above left: The table, designed by the architect, is made of steel and tempered glass, a visually light effect. Fixed lighting makes sense where floor space is restricted. Wall-mounted lights ('Tolomeo' by de Lucchi) are angled to uplight the volume of space.

entrance

kitchen

dining area

living area

bedroom

closet

bathroom

Left: The black steel girders serve as a contemporary reference to the oak beams of the Middle Ages.

ITALIAN STABLE CONVERSION 40 square metres

Above: The bench seating was custom-designed by the architect and is made of oak to match the floor. Draping the sofa in a white cover reduces its impact.

Above right: Wall cupboards and a drawer unit on top of the oak bench provide storage space in the living/dining area.

Left: The sliding glass doors screening the sleeping area comprise three elements; the central panel is fixed and the flanking sections slide across each other.

Above: The compact bathroom is fitted with beechwood units and includes a shower cabinet. A long wall mirror increases the sense of space.

Opposite: The steel and glass bedside table is a scaled down version of the dining table. A striking black, white and red artwork creates a strong focal point the all-white colour scheme.

case study
HONG KONG APARTMENT

Although spacious by Hong Kong standards, at 92 square metres, this city apartment nevertheless provides a not overly generous degree of accommodation for a family of four. Situated in a desirable location in one of Hong Kong's busiest shopping districts, the apartment has been completely remodelled to provide a serene, free-flowing oasis of calm.

The disposition of space stands conventional planning on its head. The flat was completely gutted except for a central column, around which was built a 'pavilion' housing a daybed/sofa on one side, the master bed on the other and a walk-in wardrobe between the two. Around the perimeter of the apartment runs a thick wall housing storage and the usual household amenities such as cooking, bathing and dining areas; projecting from the wall are two organic, curved capsules that enclose a lavatory and a second bathroom.

Although the central location of the apartment was a prime attraction, surrounding tower blocks make for unexciting views. The contemplative nature of the space owes much to the fact that the windows are obscured by huge panes of acid-etched glass. These allow diffused natural light to flood the interior while screening the harsh reality of the city environment. As the central pavilion stops short of the ceiling and the kitchen is raised on a platform, light penetrates to every area of the apartment and there are clear interior views from space to space.

Above and opposite: A long stone bath positioned against the perimeter wall is directly accessible from the main bedroom. The lavatory is sited within a curved enclosure that projects out into the space.

Right: The kitchen is raised up on a platform. Well-placed downlighting ensures a bright work space and floor-level lighting creates the impression that the kitchen is hovering over the floor. Cabinets, sink, hob and oven are all built into the perimeter wall.

Below: A huge pane of acid-etched glass provides a luminous backdrop to the dining area. Within these flat planes are small clear rectangles screened with hanging silk panels that can be brushed aside to provide views outside. The long bench around the dining table doubles as extra storage space.

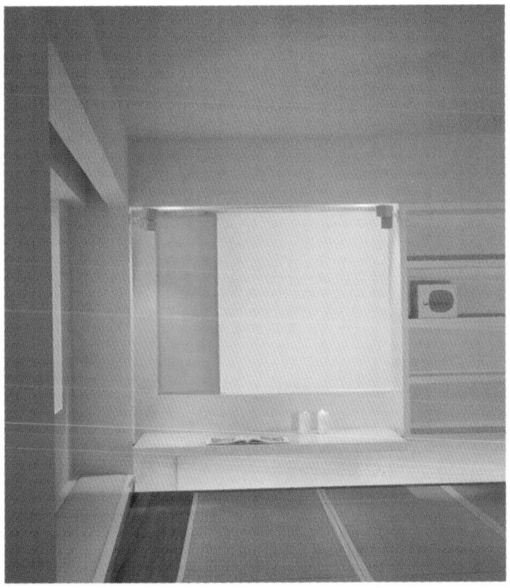

Above: The main living space opens out from the daybed in the central pavilion. Tatami mats edged in white silk are laid over reclaimed teak floorboards.

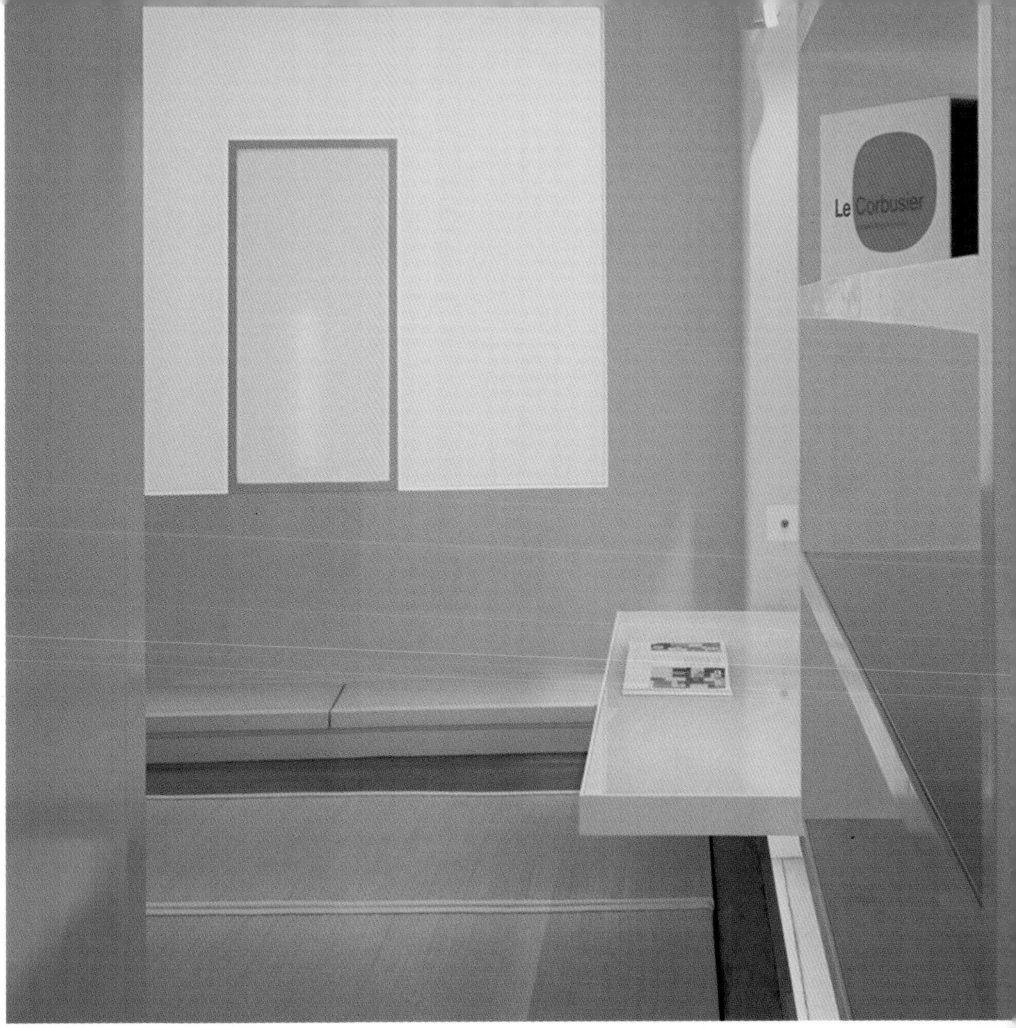
Le Corbusier

Above: An extended window ledge forms a low table for working or reading. Seamless storage fitted into the perimeter wall keeps clutter and visual distractions to an absolute minimum.

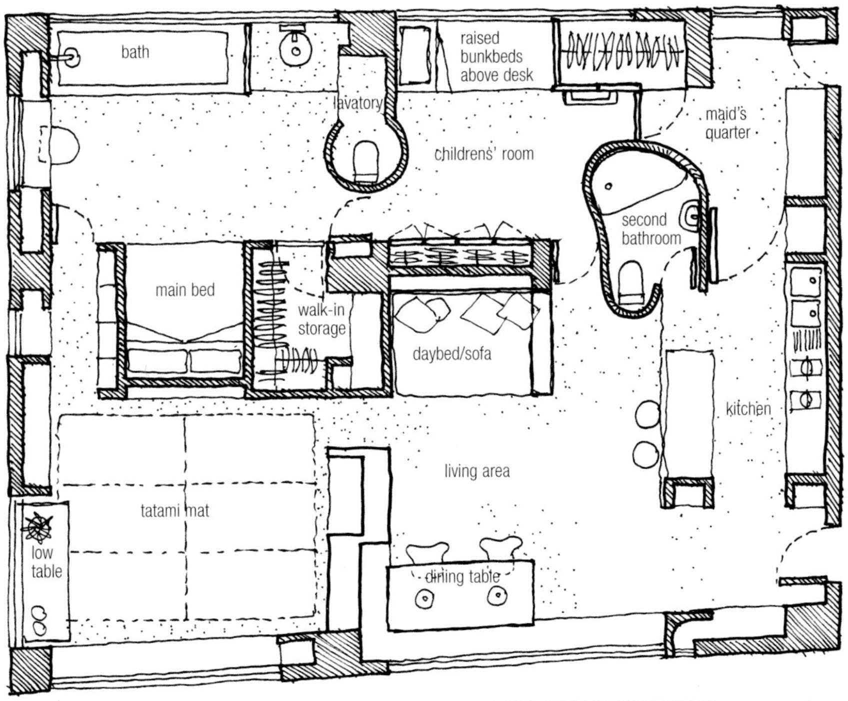
bath
lavatory
raised bunkbeds above desk
childrens' room
maid's quarter
second bathroom
main bed
walk-in storage
daybed/sofa
kitchen
living area
tatami mat
low table
dining table

HONG KONG APARTMENT 92 square metres

Left: The main bed is slotted into a box-like enclosure that forms part of the central pavilion. Shallow recesses serve as bookshelves and house concealed light sources for reading.

Opposite: A pair of bunkbeds for the children are accessed via neat stainless steel brackets set into the wall. The space beneath is fitted out with cupboards and a desk – ideal for homework.

Above: Between the bedroom and the daybed in the central pavilion is a walk-in wardrobe for extensive clothes storage. All walls and fitted features are painted in flat matt white to maximise the effect of natural light.

circulation & division

Our experience of space
is not static.

Opposite: Having it both
ways: a desk with a lift-up
top provides both a study
area with a stimulating view
and a quick and easy means
of access to the adjacent
roof terrace.

Our experience of space is not
static. During the course of a day, we move from
area to area, level to level, performing a host of
routine tasks, from fetching the post to making
the supper – even the most inert couch potato
shifts off the sofa sometimes. These little journeys
to and fro, so insignificant that they barely register
as experiences in themselves, reveal space in
another dimension. If routes are clear and
unobstructed, you will have a feeling of ease and
efficiency; if routes are awkward, they will be a
constant source of low-level frustration.

'Circulation space' is the architectural term
for stairways, halls and landings, but can be
extended to apply to any pattern of movement,
whether it is between rooms or within a room or
series of areas. In this context, it is not merely the
route to the front door that is an issue, but also
the way you arrange furnishings in a living space
or the layout of kitchen and bathroom fixtures.

In a small space, the whole issue of
circulation is particularly important. When there is
not much room in the first place, any obstacles or
difficulties you experience as you move about will
simply serve to reinforce the feeling that the
space is too small to be comfortable. In a more
positive sense, circulation can be the means of
adding richness and variety to the way you
experience a space, qualities that can go a long
way to counteract any actual limitations of size.

The counterpart of circulation is division:
how space is partitioned, whether by doors,

sliding panels, piece of furnitures or screens, will invariably direct the way you travel around within it. Here a useful point of reference, and one that was hugely influential on early proponents of the open plan, is the traditional Japanese house, with its sliding ricepaper screens. It was the interpenetration of spaces in the Japanese house that so inspired early modernists such as Charles Rennie Mackintosh and Frank Lloyd Wright, particularly the way in which different areas and levels remained connected with each other rather than existing as distinct fixed enclosures. In the Japanese house, space was conceived in modules based on the dimensions of the tatami mat, with translucent screens serving as flexible dividers between spaces and between indoors and out: part wall, part door and part window. It is a model that has an equal relevance in the design of multipurpose small spaces today.

PATTERNS OF MOVEMENT

As visitors to palaces and stately homes may be aware, the hallway or corridor is a relatively recent innovation in terms of architectural planning. In great baroque houses rooms simply opened directly onto rooms with no intermediate space to separate them. On the grandest scale, this arrangement was a means of reinforcing the hierarchy of power. As anteroom succeeded anteroom, the vistor progressed along a preordained path to the eventual destination, the ultimate seat of authority, with the favoured allowed to pass through from the outer public areas into the inner sanctum itself. The influence of classicism arranged such sequences in the dramatic symmetrical vista of the enfilade. Needless to say, privacy as we understand it today was unknown. Servants often slept within the chambers of those they attended, not in some remote quarter, attic or wing.

By the eighteenth century, with increased prosperity and the emergence of an upper middle class, the country house lost some of its palatial overtones and a new, more domestic ideal was born. With it came the need to separate areas to provide intimate enclaves and a clear distinction between sexes and classes, a segregation subsequently taken to extremes in Victorian and Edwardian country houses. Multiple stairways and interminable corridors created a honeycomb of pathways, providing alternative routes where servants could creep about unseen by those whom they served. In some cases, a similar approach was adopted in the surrounding gardens and parks, with trenches dug across lawns so that gardeners could cross from one side to the other without 'spoiling' the view. I always remember the story of a rather grand lady visiting the home of a less wealthy friend. 'How beautiful those yellow autumn leaves look lying on the grass,' she remarked. 'Does your gardener scatter them there every morning?'

In humbler surroundings circulation areas were also somewhat disproportionate. In the typical Victorian terraced house the huge return of the staircase devours space, and hallways, landings and stairs combined can account for a considerable percentage of a house's entire volume. A waste of space, we might well think. But in this context, it is worth looking at the work of Sir Edwin Lutyens, an architect who understood spatial conundrums better than most. Lutyens was the designer most favoured by the Edwardian nouveau riche, clients who had made their money in trade or stockbroking and who were looking to put down roots in the country –

albeit preferably in a location a commutable distance from town. What Lutyens was able to achieve, whether he was working in a vernacular Arts and Crafts idiom or in the classical style of his later period, were houses that flattered the social and aesthetic aspirations of his clients by seeming bigger than they actually were. He accomplished this chiefly through the design of circulation space.

Lutyens has been much criticized, even in his own lifetime, for the sheer indulgence of his stairs, halls, vestibules, landings and corridors. He arranged such connections so that they did not travel the shortest distance between two points, but took what one might call the 'scenic route' and offered a choice of directions; his landings

and galleries were room-sized; his staircases were broad and sweeping. Houses were laid out around internal courtyards or concealed within them generous voids. The effect was to transform the prosaic fact of moving through a house into a rich spatial event, with surprise and anticipation built into the experience.

Just how pleasurable these experiences were can be judged by the response of the great English gardener Gertrude Jekyll, for whom Lutyens built one of his first important houses. The house, Munstead Wood, has a broad first-floor gallery leading to the bedrooms, lit along one side by a series of casement windows. 'In some mysterious way [the gallery] is imbued with an expression of cheerful, kindly welcome, of

Above: The informality of the contemporary lifestyle has broken down the barriers that used to exist between hard-working areas such as kitchens and places where people gather to relax or entertain. Here the detailing of the cooking end of the room is extended to the dining area to provide an element of visual unity.

restfulness to mind and body, of abounding satisfaction to eye and brain,' wrote Miss Jekyll. She chose the bedroom at the far end of the gallery to be her own, just to ensure the daily pleasure of walking the length of it.

Lutyens believed that it was 'the waste of space that, unwittingly, creates that most valuable asset, the gain of space'. The generosity, wit and theatricality of these circulation patterns provided both the illusion of space and a constant source of animation.

In many respects, this idea is an extension of 'hazard and surprise', a guiding design principle of one of my favourite architects, Sir John Soane.

Above: A full-height sliding partition provides a flexible way of screening space. When doorways or partitions extend from floor to ceiling, the effect is to subdivide space in such a way that it does not necessarily read as a sequence of conventional rooms – and sliding doors are inherently space-saving.

Opposite below: This sequence of interlinked spaces serves as a contemporary version of the old classical idea of 'enfilade', providing a linking view through from area to area. The red wall at the far end of the space designates a shower area, where water drains directly through the slatted wood floor. A further change of flooring, from mosaic to wood signals the shift from the bathing area to the bedroom.

His house-cum-museum in Lincoln's Inn Fields in London is a masterpiece of spatial ambiguity, where contrasting volumes, vistas and mirrored surfaces both confuse and enchant the eye.

What such examples have to teach us is that size, to a large extent, is in the eye of the beholder and that there is room, even in the most confined surroundings, for an element of delight. Any space – whether it is indoors or out – that can be read as a whole from a single vantage point will be dull. But if you have to move through it in order for every aspect to be revealed, if there are hidden corners, sudden contrasts or an unfolding view, there is less opportunity for staleness to creep in.

CIRCULATION IN SMALL SPACES

Circulation in small spaces can be an important unifying device, simplifying and clarifying routes so that maximum living area is achieved. At the same time, as the work of Lutyens and Soane demonstrates, these patterns can also play a key role in our enjoyment of space and even trick us into thinking there's more than meets the eye. The art is to reconcile the two sides of the issue.

Above: Translucent pivoting panels make an unobtrusive screen for a bedroom within an open-plan space. Screens made of perspex or ricepaper provide a fair degree of privacy but do not block precious natural light.

To begin with, you should make a quick assessment of how you move about from area to area. If you have lived somewhere for a while, patches of wear on the floor can be very revealing of common traffic routes. Are there tight corners where you feel you have to squeeze past? Are there any obstacles in your way – doors that open into your path or pieces of furniture that you are always bumping into? How easy is it to bring in the shopping or take out the rubbish?

On the most basic, remedial level, circulation can be vastly improved simply by removing obstacles to make a clear route. Hallways and landings can usefully serve as storage areas if they are wide enough, but in the majority of cases furnishings should be kept to an absolute minimum. In many households, too, there's a tendency for halls and stairs to silt up with clutter, forming an unofficial dumping ground for unanswered post, sports kit, things on their way out or things on their way in. A clean sweep of such detritus and a firm no-dumping policy can provide psychological as well as physical breathing space.

In other cases, however, it may be obvious that the awkwardness is more in-built. Look at the way doors are hung. Would it improve matters if a door was rehung to open the other way or replaced with a sliding panel? Is there more than one entrance to an area and, if so, which do you use? Redundant doorways can be easily blocked off to create additional wall space.

A scale drawing or sketch plan is a useful aid when it comes to replanning circulation in a more radical manner, providing a degree of abstraction from the here and now which helps to analyze problems and suggest solutions. Like the symmetrical enfilade of the baroque house, a

clear, straight route from the front to the back, from the entrance to the garden, for example, can serve as an axis that multiplies the sense of space by leading the eye onwards. Another possibility might be to arrange circulation centrally, with a lobby or hall providing access to stairs to upper levels. In both cases, there is the potential to draw in natural light, either through windows, glazed doors or skylights, and add to the quality of expansiveness. Slivers of light or views that appear in unexpected places as you move about from place to place imbue circulation areas with an all-important sense of animation.

The staircase is one of the most critical circulation spaces of all. In older properties, the stairs are likely to be fairly ponderously detailed and can occupy a vast amount of space. In situations where they are legally permissable, open stairways, such as spiral stairs or steps cantilevered from the wall, are welcome additions to small spaces, since they do not block light and views as you move from level to level. Their additional bonus is sheer theatricality, an element that can otherwise be somewhat lacking.

WALLS & PARTITIONS

Replanning circulation often entails moving walls and dividing space in new ways. In confined surroundings, even quite minimal changes can make all the difference, especially to fitted areas such as bathrooms and kitchens. Gaining an extra few centimetres by pulling a wall forward into a hallway, for example, can ease matters sufficiently to allow a workable layout.

Adding partition walls is a relatively straightforward process, with no structural implications. The main factors to consider are appropriate siting and access. When you are

Opposite: For structural reasons, it is not always possible to remove all portions of existing walls, particularly where these have a supporting role to play. In this conversion, large openings have been created to open out views internally and provide a suggestion of an open-plan arrangement. The result: what had formerly been a conventional hallway now reads as part of the space as a whole.

dividing one large space to make two smaller ones, pay attention to existing architectural features such as windows and chimney breasts so that the resulting new spaces are well-proportioned and properly lit. If you are creating two new bedrooms, each will need its own independent access, which may result in a loss of usable floor area when you come to juggle the circulation.

But not all partitions need be solid walls. In situations where you want to maintain openness while providing an element of enclosure for differerent activities, half-height or half-width partitions are useful allies and will not compromise the fundamental qualities of the space as a whole. A half-width partition can serve to screen a working area from the rest of a bedroom, for example, so that the two very different functions of the space do not conflict. To maximize natural light, such partitions can be constructed of glass bricks or other translucent materials. In the same way, half-height partitions such as waist-level counters provide an effective means of delineating a kitchen area, while preserving its connection with the rest of the household. Another related strategy is to construct a dividing wall that falls short of the

Above and right: Partitions that do not extend the full height or width of a space can still make very effective dividers, with the bonus of preserving views and making the most of available light. Here a beautifully detailed wooden divider serves to anchor the arrangement of bed and bedside tables on one side, while defining a study area on the other.

Left: The simple strategy of opening out a conventional staircase and hallway by removing a portion of the flanking wall increases the overall sense of spaciousness although no actual floor area has been gained.

Right: An open stairway and mezzanine level provide a significant amount of extra room without compromising the sense of volume in this double-height space.

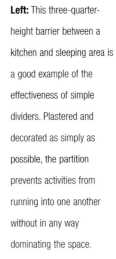

Left: This three-quarter-height barrier between a kitchen and sleeping area is a good example of the effectiveness of simple dividers. Plastered and decorated as simply as possible, the partition prevents activities from running into one another without in any way dominating the space.

ceiling and acts essentially as a large free-standing panel. This type of division can be a good way of providing privacy for a sleeping area within an open-plan layout.

Solid walls or partitions of any description do not necessarily need to be straight. Although, as any builder will tell you, curves are more costly to construct, there are many instances where the gentle sweep of a partition wall can introduce a pleasing sculptural quality.

FLEXIBLE DIVISIONS

Small spaces are often called upon to work in different ways at different times – to accommodate guests staying for the weekend, to double as live/work areas or to alternate between public and private roles at a moment's notice. Multipurpose spaces call for flexibility in terms of the way they are subdivided.

In this instance, the trick is to consider the space as a complete entity, with divisions allowing a variety of permutations in terms of layout. Certain spatial strategies can be very useful when it comes to reinforcing this perception. One is to substitute floor-to-ceiling sliding panels for doors, so that different areas can be opened or enclosed at will. Such panels, by doing away with the door 'head' – or the portion of wall over a doorway – allow the ceiling and floor planes to run through a space unobstructed, which in itself enhances space by introducing a sense of calming geometry. If you get rid of the notion of the 'door', you also get rid of the notion of the room as a container.

Similar sliding panels can be used to screen built-in kitchens or bathrooms and prevent functional areas from dominating a living space between the times when they are in use. At their most ingenious, panels can be constructed as

Above: Two sides of the same coin: a half-height partition between a bedroom and bathroom is finished with mosaic tiling on the bathroom side and serves as a backrest for bench seating on the other.

Opposite: Sliding full-height glass panels screen off kitchen activity from the rest of the household.

modules containing fold-down beds or swung out to reconfigure an existing layout to provide extra sleeping accommodation.

Needless to say, a similar type of flexible partitioning can be achieved with portable screens, free-standing room dividers and even the placement of furniture. Screens introduce a certain sculptural quality and can be moved about as the need arises. Dividers interrupt a space physically without blocking light or views and double up as places for storage and display. At the most minimal, an implicit division of space can be achieved simply with furniture and furnishings. The back of a sofa placed across the middle of a space can effectively mark the boundary between a living area and a working or dining area, just as a large rug can anchor a seating arrangement within a larger space.

FIXED LAYOUTS

With some rooms, flexible divisions are just not possible. Kitchens, bathrooms and utility areas require fixed points of servicing, which, in turn, commit you to a more or less fixed layout. Sinks, showers, baths and washing machines must be plumbed in; cookers, hobs and ovens need gas or electrical supply; large appliances such as refrigerators and freezers do not lend themselves to flexible arrangement. It is possible to maximize space in such hard-working areas by opting for small-scale fixtures and fittings, but often this merely compromises efficiency to an unacceptable degree. Careful planning to make the best possible use of space, together with a little lateral thinking, will generally result in a better solution all round.

The science of ergonomics grew out of time and motion studies designed to improve the efficiency of assembly-line production by mimimizing the effort it took to carry out repetitive tasks. This, in turn, depended on a thorough analysis of common human capabilities. But while factories have become more and more mechanized, even roboticized, cooking in its fullest sense remains a physical activity. Of course, setting the microwave or ordering a takeway exercises little more than the odd button-pressing finger or two. Nevertheless, preparing an average meal still entails a variety of related gestures and movements, from bending and reaching, to walking back and forth between sink, fridge, hob and oven.

What such research demonstrated, and what has become accepted wisdom for kitchen planners ever since, is that the most efficient kitchen layout is one where the distances between the main areas of activity are not too great – a few paces at the maximum. This notion, enshrined in the concept of the 'work triangle' – where the three points of the triangle equate to the cold zone of the refrigerator, the wet zone of the sink and preparation area and the hot zone of the cooker, hob or oven – applies whatever form the kitchen layout subsequently takes.

However, you do not need a thorough understanding of ergonomics to appreciate the obvious: routine tasks such as fetching ingredients from the refrigerator, freezer or store cupboard, and washing, preparing and cooking them, are best performed with the mimimum of to-ing and fro-ing and where routes are clear and unobstructed. All this is good news for keen cooks with little space at their disposal, although it is perhaps not such good news for those cooks enamoured of kitchenalia – what a small kitchen

Left: Metal panels suspended from industrial-style tracking make an effective screen for a kitchen arranged 'in line' along the length of a wall, the robust aesthetic in keeping with the warehouse setting.

KITCHENS

Ergonomic studies of kitchenwork were first carried out as long ago as the nineteenth century, although it was well into the twentieth century before such findings were put into common practice. The purpose of such research – to determine the most efficient work sequence and hence kitchen layout – had a heightened importance between the wars, at a time when domestic help was becoming increasingly scarce. After the Second World War, when the servant class more or less disappeared completely, it was clear that the modern kitchen was to be largely a one-person operation.

Above: A variation on the U-shaped layout, this small kitchen is tightly planned for maximum efficiency. Kitchens are less tiring to work in when distances are not too great between hot, cold and wet 'zones'.

Right: Internal 'windows' cut into a partition wall provide a tantalizing glimpse of kitchen activity beyond.

definitely cannot accommodate is innumerable gadgets. Every cook should ask themselves if they really need and use all the clutter they surround themselves with.

With the work triangle as the basis, a number of different types of layout serve equally well in a small space. Which type of layout you adopt will depend on the precise nature of the space at your disposal and whether you have to work within existing constraints or have the opportunity to design an entire space from scratch.

Many of the most workable small kitchens are variations on the galley theme, with kitchen fittings and worksurfaces arranged on either side of what is essentially a gangway. The galley itself can take the form of a cul-de-sac, an open-ended hallway connecting to other areas in the home, or a working wall of fittings and fixtures screened by a preparation counter within an open-plan space. In all cases, the basic layout is the same and the

potential for tight planning is maximized.

Another simple form of kitchen layout is the in-line layout, where everything is aligned along one wall. One particular advantage of this arrangement, especially in an open-plan space, is that it makes it easier for the entire kitchen area to be screened from view when not in use. A number of manufacturers now produce off-the-peg kitchens in a single prefabricated unit containing all the essential fittings and appliances, and which can

all the main types of kitchen layout, the island is perhaps the least suited to a small space since it effectively requires double the space of a galley.

BATHROOMS

When I was just starting out as a designer, one of the first places I ever lived in London was a miserably damp basement flat near Primrose Hill. One of its more eccentric features – although it was far from uncommon at the time – was the fact that the bathtub was located on one side of the kitchen. I used to put a lid over the bath so I could use the surface as a place to prepare food – or have a bath while supper was cooking, stirring and soaping in unison!

This rather primitive arrangement, essentially a plumbed-in version of the old tin bath in front of the kitchen range, does, however, illustrate an important point about bathroom layout and that is the fact that lavatories and bathtubs do not necessarily need to be yoked together, although they both serve fundamental bodily functions and both require the same sort of servicing.

One of the first decisions you should make about bathroom layout is whether separating the two would make a better use of space. Really tiny bathrooms, where the lavatory, handbasin and tub are cheek-by-jowl can be fairly unpleasant places; on the other hand, two small rooms, one for a lavatory and one for a shower, may occupy no more floor area but offer certain practical and psychological advantages. Then, again, there is no reason why bathing should not be incorporated within a sleeping area provided the servicing can be made to work. A sunken bath or shower stall in a corner of a bedroom takes the 'en-suite' idea just that little bit further and underscores the basic connection between washing and relaxing.

simply be slotted, plugged and plumbed into place. These compact 'kitchens-in-a-box' are simply a compressed version of the in-line layout. It has to be said, however, that most serious cooks find in-line layouts somewhat frustrating, especially where the line is fairly extended.

Other common kitchen layouts include the U-shaped, the L-shaped and the island. U-shaped layouts provide both comfortable working conditions – as the work triangle is implicit in the basic form of the 'U' – and the potential for each main area of activity to be served by its own area of worksurface which adds to the practicality. A further advantage is that the open end of the layout makes a convenient location for table and chairs. The L-shaped layout is broadly similar; the shorter arm of the 'L' can function as a breakfast bar/counter and as a means of partially screening the kitchen from view. Island layouts, where a central unit, table or work station serves as a cooking or preparation area, have become increasingly popular over the years. However, of

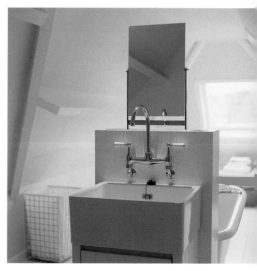

Left and below: Lack of head height under the eaves inspired this unusual but highly effective bathroom layout, with sink and bath placed centrally in the space and benefiting from shared drainage. There's something uniquely luxurious about a centrally positioned bath, and this roll-top clawfoot tub is good-looking enough to bear the scrutiny.

If you simply have no choice but to stick with the single room option, one solution is to maximize floor area by treating the entire bathroom space as a wet room – which, of course, entails waterproofing throughout, by tiling, for example. Shower heads can be installed flush with the ceiling and so that they drain directly to a sinkhole in the floor.

In a small bathroom, a matter of a few centimetres in either direction can make all the difference between ease and discomfort. You need to allow space not only for the fittings themselves, but also a margin for clear access – enough room so that you don't bang your elbows on the wall when you are leaning over the sink to wash your hair or so that you can get in and out of the bath safely. When space is severely limited, there's always a temptation to opt for small-scale versions of basic fittings and fixtures in an attempt to squeeze it all in. Better by far is to take a sideways step: a shower is infinitely preferable to a small bath in which you can't actually lie down. Wall-hung lavatory pans and sinks allow more clear floor area than pedestal varieties. Heated towel rails provide dual-function storage and heating or an alternative is to wrap towel rails around a vertical wall-hung radiator.

For most of us, the bathroom remains a private place. But even if you are a devotee of the pleasures of communal bathing, others who visit

your home may well not be quite so broadminded. This means that bathrooms, unlike kitchens, need to be separated in some way from the rest of the home. Conventional doors often compromise a tightly planned bathroom layout: either they open inwards, colliding with a sink or tub, or they open outwards into a hallway, which can create an unnecessary obstacle. Sliding doors, panels or screens make much better dividers. If you have the opportunity to create a bathroom from scratch, curved partitions can be very effective, introducing a new architectural dynamic that goes some way to alleviating any sense of enclosure. Curved walls are particularly appropriate as a means of screening a shower.

Above: A glazed panel separates a bedroom from the adjacent bathroom. At the flick of a switch, the glass changes from fully transparent to translucent, creating privacy in the bathing area and an atmospheric backdrop in the bedroom.

Opposite: A tiny window set into the wall of a shower enclosure frames a view of St Paul's Cathedral, London.
Left and above: Grouping services in a central core simplifies drainage arrangements. There's no need for partitions to be conventionally shaped. Here, the interior of the core houses a bathroom, while a kitchen area is wrapped around the outside.

case study
LONDON BASEMENT FLAT

Right: The south-facing main living space incorporates a dining area in front of a large window overlooking the terrace. The doorway to the right was opened up as part of the redesign to link the indoor and outdoor spaces.

This compact flat occupies part of the lower ground floor of a large south-facing villa in North London. The house was originally designed in about 1820 by Thomas Cubitt, architect and developer of substantial areas of Regency London, including parts of Belgravia, Bloomsbury, Islington and Camden Town. The space, which altogether amounts to around 50 square metres, has been reconfigured to make the most of existing features, employing only a minimal degree of intervention and alteration.

The principal spatial change has been to move the kitchen from its former location – where the bedroom is currently sited – to a new position, creating a working wall at one end of the main living area. The bathroom has been shortened and refitted as a shower room, freeing up extra space on either side for hanging clothes and storage. The result of these changes has been to simplify circulation routes dramatically and to link the smaller areas of the flat with the large, square main space in a continuous flow.

Because the flat has a sheltered, southerly aspect and the original walls are very thick, the one small radiator in the bathroom is enough to heat the entire space in all but the most severe weather conditions. The thick walls also provide opportunities to build in storage for books. With its easy transitions from area to area and adjacent outdoor terrace, the flat now provides a relaxed and light-filled setting for contemporary living.

Above: The kitchen was deliberately designed so as not to intrude on the main living space. To minimize its impact, there is no shelving above the worksurface and no tiled splashback. The plinth at the base of the kitchen units can be removed for access to extra storage.

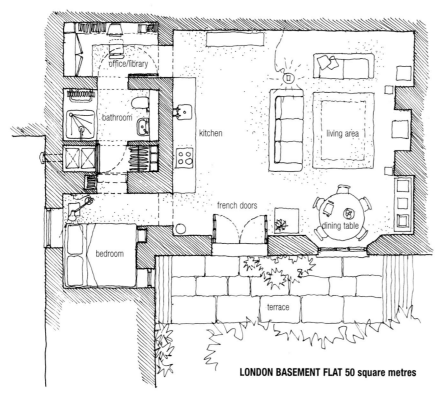

office/library

bathroom

kitchen

french doors

living area

dining table

bedroom

terrace

LONDON BASEMENT FLAT 50 square metres

Above: Detail of the bedside corner showing book storage in the adjacent transitional space. The bed space is tucked under the broad steps to the raised ground floor entrance of the main house.

Opposite, below left and right: Improved circulation means that the different areas in the flat now work as an interlinked sequence, rather than as separate self-contained boxes.

Right: The bedroom receives light in the morning and evening, critical times of the day for a sleeping area. The window also provides a useful vantage point for spotting visitors.

Left: Space for hanging clothes has been gained by making the bathroom area smaller.

Opposite: A storage and study area has been created on the other side of the bathroom. Because both of the doors accessing the bathroom are kept open in day-to-day use, there is a choice of routes from area to area, an important factor in reducing the potential for claustrophobia. The same strategy means that these smaller areas of the flat remain connected to the main space and feel much larger as a consequence.

case study
TOP-FLOOR PARIS STUDIO

Clever partitioning of space segregates different areas of activity in this tiny, top-floor flat in Paris. With a total floor area of just 27 square metres, planning assumes a critical importance. Because a small balcony runs the entire length of the apartment, providing a wonderful vantage point from which to enjoy views over the Paris rooftops and Sacré Coeur, space has been divided to make the most of the stunning panorama and available light.

The plan of the entire apartment reveals the ingenuity with which space has been maximized. Old partitions and the ceiling were stripped away to reveal a single space defined by the sloping lines of the mansard roof. The bedroom area is centrally placed. A wall finished in neutral-coloured waxed cement serves as a combined bedhead and screen for the bathroom and lavatory on the other side. At the foot of the bed is a half-height divider, finished in plywood. Housing a television for bedtime viewing, the divider screens the bed from the living room end of the apartment. Within the living space, a small kitchen area is housed behind louvred wooden doors so that it can be closed off when not in use.

To maximize the light, airy quality of the little studio, surfaces and finishes have been kept deliberately soft and neutral in tone. But material contrasts – zinc and concrete, steel and plywood – add a lively tactile quality that adds a sense of character and charm.

Above: A small balcony, crammed with pots and plants, provides a romantic view of the rooftops of Paris.

Opposite: Space has been subdivided so that all areas of the studio benefit from light and views. The sloping lines of the mansard roof are panelled in tongue-and-groove and painted white. The bathroom is situated on the other side of the wall that serves as the bedhead.

Above: A neutral palette of materials enhances the sense of space. Tinted and waxed cement makes a svelte surface for the wall dividing the bedroom area from the bathroom; the projecting plane serves as a bedhead and a convenient ledge for decorative display.

Right: The half-height divider at the foot of the bed is finished in plywood and incorporates useful storage niches for the audio and visual equipment.

Right: On the other side of the partition wall from the bed is a sink and shower accessed via an open entranceway. The stainless steel basin is housed in a cement-finished unit, sealed to make it waterproof; the consistency of the finish contributes to the seamless quality of the design.

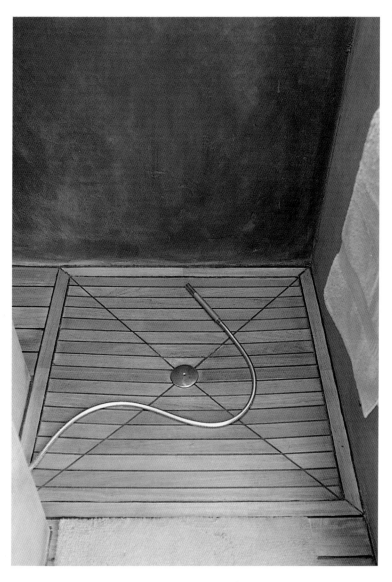

Left: The shower, floored in water-resistant hardwood, drains directly to the floor, another space-saving and clutter-free feature.

White-painted louvred doors conceal a compact kitchen area neatly integrated at one end of the living space. The kitchen is fully fitted with sink, hob and oven, with deep shelves above for crockery and cookware.

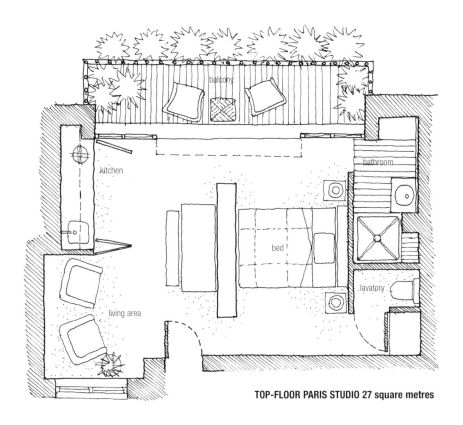

TOP-FLOOR PARIS STUDIO 27 square metres

Above: When floor area is limited, space-saving strategies such as mounting televisions on wall brackets are a good idea.

Right: The tiny balcony is constructed of zinc and rustic teak and provides just enough space for a couple of chairs and a few pots and containers.

light & air

'A house is only habitable
when it is full of light and air.'

Le Corbusier

A house is only habitable when it is full of light and air,' wrote Le Corbusier in *Towards a New Architecture* (1923). Elsewhere in the same book, he defines the house as 'a receptacle for light and sun' and rails against the dull, dingy nineteenth-century interior, shrouded in thick drapery and crammed with dust-catching ornaments and furnishings, in tones of utmost disgust and revulsion.

Today, light and air seem so fundamental to our well-being that it is hard to imagine how radical Le Corbusier's ideas were at the time, or the degree of opposition he faced in conventional circles. The Victorian period still cast its shadow over the early decades of the twentieth century; modern technology, which has brought us central heating, electric light and household appliances, was still in its infancy. In the nineteenth century and for some while after, light was treated almost like an intruder. There was the concern that excessive sunlight would fade fine fabrics and finishes; at the same time, in those days of open fires and gas lighting, sombre decorative schemes were a common sense solution when walls and fabrics quickly became discoloured with smoke and fumes.

Practical matters, however, cannot account entirely for the Victorian attitude to light. There was also the sense that openness and transparency were somehow not quite genteel. By contrast, in the eighteenth century, when issues of fading and discoloration were no less relevant, light-filled interiors were actively

Above: In terraced houses, where there are windows only on the front and side walls, it can be difficult to light halls and stairways adequately. Here, a curved skylight in a vaulted roof is precisely positioned to spill light down the staircase to lower levels. Recessed downlights around the perimeter of the skylight serve as background lighting after nightfall.

Above: A precisely judged opening cut into a partition between kitchen and eating areas allows light from the windows to spill into the dining area.

Opposite: A fully glazed timber-framed enclosure for a staircase at the rear of this house brings light into two levels and dramatically opens out the lower ground floor.

preferred, perhaps as the almost literal expression of an age of reason or 'enlightenment'.

Le Corbusier believed that light and air were necessary for human health and to promote conditions of good hygiene. But, in progressive design, these elements have come to symbolize something more – the blurring of boundaries between indoors and out, the fundamental need to create connections with the natural world, even a sense of honesty and unpretentiousness. Aided by advances in glass technology, buildings such as Philip Johnson's Glass House in New Canaan, USA (1949), with its transparent external walls,

provide the ultimate realization of such ideals.

Light is one of the most important elements in the contemporary design vocabulary. But it is also deeply associated with the sense of feeling good in one's skin. While people have always instinctively known that sunshine lifts the spirits, in recent decades the widespread availability of cheap air travel to dependably sunny shores has only heightened the connection: light means fun, freedom and happiness.

Light, and its partner shadow, describe and reveal the interior. The other intangible element – air – sensed chiefly in terms of air movement,

literally breathes life into a space. The smaller the area, the greater the need for light and air in all their subtle manifestations.

MAKING THE MOST OF NATURAL LIGHT

It is an instinctive human response to gravitate towards the light. With sight our dominant sense, light enables us to orientate ourselves and to read and appreciate our surroundings. But light is also inherently sociable and welcoming: it cheers us up. Darkness, by contrast, is our security blanket, or the comforter we wrap round ourselves when feeling threatened or blue.

It is not merely the sheer presence of light that is so uplifting. Where light comes in, so do views and these extend our sense of space beyond the immediate confines of the interior. Think about two small hotel rooms, each the same size and each furnished and decorated in exactly the same way. One has a window with a view of the sea; the other has a window with a view of a brick wall. Which one could you stay in longer?

Above and left: Many older houses have a relatively poor quality of natural light in circulation spaces. Here, a series of translucent acrylic risers set into the top of a staircase provide an innovative way of letting light into a windowless understairs cloakroom.

Opposite: Two large internal windows serve as an elegant transparent partition between a bedroom and the rest of the space. Simple pull-down roller blinds provide privacy at nighttime.

Small spaces often have certain in-built disadvantages when it comes to natural light. If your home is a basement flat or forms part of a terraced property, the possibilities of light coming from different directions, particularly from above, may be limited. Even industrial or commercial conversions, especially those lofts that are not on the topmost storey of a building, may also suffer in this respect. Yet in small spaces the need for light is acute. Good lighting, both natural and artificial, is one of the best ways of making a space seem bigger than it actually is.

The first step is to make a preliminary assessment of the lighting conditions in each area of your home. Look at where light falls and note how it changes throughout the day. It is not enough simply to note the basic orientation of each area. Natural light is not an even source that emanates from a single direction, nor is it akin to electric light which can be switched on and off at whim: it is full of vitality because it is constantly changing. The mobility of light – at different times of the day, in different weather conditions, at different seasons – is part of what makes it so enchanting. Sitting under a tree on a sunny day, you will experience minute variations as the light filters through the leaves dappling the ground. The design of interior spaces should make the most of this inherent changeability.

One architect who fully appreciated the changeability of natural light and its role in animating the interior was Charles Rennie Mackintosh. At The Hill House in Scotland, Mackintosh's finest domestic scheme, a sunny, south-facing bay occupies one end of the drawing room, with a window seat overlooking the garden. For this location Mackintosh designed a small square table, whose base is a complex

intersecting network of open squares. As the sun moves across the sky during the day, the shadows cast by the open fretwork of the table base shift across the floor like a beautiful abstract picture, adding a sense of dynamism and life.

ORIENTATION

A basic way to improve the quality of light is to arrange living spaces to make the most of orientation. This may be simply a matter of

Above: Ceiling-height, sliding partitions made of frosted glass create an airy en-suite bathroom in this compact, minimal bedroom.

Above: The dividers bisect a large round window and, although it is generally inadvisable to divide a window in this way, the glazed screen avoids a heavy or clumsy effect.

juggling the layout so that the areas where you spend most time and where you tend to socialize are those where the conditions of natural light are at their best. In the northern hemisphere, south- or west-facing areas will be sunnier and warmer than those facing north or east.

Conventional planning tends to site living spaces at ground or first floor level, with bedrooms on the levels above. But in built-up urban areas, the quality of light at upper levels is

OPENINGS

In some cases, the only way of directly improving the quality of light is to enlarge existing external openings or to add new ones. As discussed on page 43–46, such work generally has structural implications and is not to be undertaken lightly, but the results can be well worth the effort and expense. A standard improvement is to turn a single door or window at ground level into double doors to increase available light and provide access to a garden. A more radical and contemporary version of the same idea would be to remove the entire wall and fit the opening with a single glazed panel that pivots, slides or raises up.

If there is the opportunity, adding a window on a wall that flanks an existing opening will immensely improve spatial quality: light coming from two directions immediately creates a sense of expansiveness. There's often no need to limit yourself to standard shapes or sizes. Long, narrow windows make a dramatic counterpoint to a double-height space; portholes provide a focal point.

Above: A round skylight provides natural lighting over a kitchen preparation area. Reflective stainless steel surfaces and a translucent screen multiply the effect.
Right: Pavement lights provide evocative toplighting for a shower area in a basement flat.

generally much better than in lower or semi-basement levels which are likely to be heavily overshadowed by neighbouring buildings. Shifting living and kitchen areas up to the top, with bedrooms, where sunlight is not so valuable, relegated to lower levels can make a dramatic difference to the way space is experienced. It is important to bear in mind, however, that the opportunity to connect living areas on upper levels with outdoor spaces is much more limited. If your garden is little more than a paved yard or if you have none at all, it won't be much of a sacrifice; otherwise, you may wish to add an external stair to provide access or open out the upper level to create an adjoining roof terrace.

Toplighting in the form of skylights or glazed roofs can be one of the most effective ways of opening up a small space, literally lifting off the lid and creating the illusion of greater spatial volume. Toplighting reveals pure sky, a calming infinite view, and exposes a space to natural light variations like no other form of window. Siting is critical. Skylights work well positioned directly over a bath or bed – vantage points where you will naturally be in a position to lie back and appreciate the view. In a similar way, a skylight over a stairwell leads the eye up through a space and spills light down to lower levels. A more ambitious form of toplighting is to create an internal atrium or courtyard. This brings light in not only from above, but potentially from each side as well, creating new internal views and vistas.

Choice of glass is an important consideration when creating new openings or glazing a roof. Advances in technology have resulted in the development of shatterproof,

Above left: Coloured glass panels running the length of a corridor provide a diffused source of gentle illumination.
Above: Glazed roof lights dramatically positioned over a glass and metal mesh stairway spill light down from level to level. Toplighting is effective because it evokes the experience of being outdoors on a sunny day.

solution. These are best used with conviction, as a generous infill or even to create an entire glazed wall. For smaller openings, frosted or etched glass can provide a similar degree of opacity.

Improving external openings or adding new ones may not serve to bring light into all areas of the home. Where a space is very long and narrow, for example, natural light may well not penetrate to the heart of it. Here the solution may be to punch through walls and create internal windows that serve to spill light through from area to area. Unlike external openings, internal windows need not be glazed and may not entail structural alteration. In partition walls, they can take any form you choose: square apertures, long horizontal or vertical strips, or portholes will animate adjoining areas with light and slices of views. A similar effect can be achieved by replacing solid partitions with glazing or, if you prefer a little less transparency, with a translucent material such as glass brick, perspex, wire mesh, ricepaper, fabric or whatever allows a degree of light to shine through.

This type of strategy can be extended to bring light down through a space. The use of glass as a flooring material offers the potential to create a theatrical sense of space, with light flowing from level to level. Glass staircases provide the ultimate in drama; glass mezzanine walkways maintain the sense of space in an area that is vertically divided. Small portions of glass flooring strategically placed can also extend the effect of toplighting to lower levels. The type of glass suitable for flooring applications is thick, annealed float glass; each floor must be specified according to loading requirements and sandblasted friction bars are generally necessary to prevent slipping. Less costly, and a little less nerve-wracking for the fainthearted, is flooring made of strong metal mesh or castiron grating.

Above: Glass bricks and blocks offer another way of introducing light into the interior without compromising security or privacy. A particular bonus is the rippled, watery quality of the light and shadow. Glass bricks should ideally be used generously to infill large openings or make substantial partitions or dividers.

toughened glass that is every bit as strong as an equivalent masonry wall; this type of glass should always be used in situations where there is a security or safety implication. Glass is also now available with a special insulating coating that prevents excessive heat gain in summer or heat loss in winter, ideal for glazed roofs or glazed entensions. Alternatively, double- or triple-glazed windows can be made to individual specification; types are available that contain adjustable blinds sandwiched between the glass layers. If you want more light, but not at the expense of your privacy, translucent glass bricks can provide a good

Left: A large internal window counteracts any feeling of enclosure for a compact kitchen. Sliding partitions allow the room to be totally closed off when required.

Above: Glass floors provide an unbeatable sense of drama. All four edges of glass panels need to be fully enclosed and supported by a cushioning element; friction bars may also be required to prevent slipping.

Left: Irregular shaped cutouts in partition walls provide intriguing views as you move about from place to place or level to level.

MIRROR

Mirror is an excellent way of multiplying the effect of both natural and artificial light and of creating the illusion of space through false perspectives. It also needs to be handled with a degree of sensitivity – used too much and the effect can be rather reminiscent of a fairground attraction.

A sheet of mirror covering one wall of a small space is an invaluable means of counteracting a sense of confinement. Most lifts have a mirrored surface to quell the fears of those who would be too claustrophobic to ride up and down in a small moving box. Similarly, placing a mirror opposite another mirror can set up an infinity of views.

One of the best uses of mirror in a small space is to reflect sunlight into areas that would otherwise be dark. Placing a mirror at right-angles to a window, or opposite a window or door, can be almost as effective as creating another opening. Slivers of angled mirror placed round a window in the Soanian manner throw light forwards into a room and make the window appear larger than it actually is.

SCREENING

Exhibitionists (and applicants to Big Brother) excepted, most people do not wish to live their entire lives in full view, which means that windows and other openings will need to be screened from time to time. Elaborate curtains or window treatments with fussy detailing such as pelmets add an unnecessary level of detail in a small space. It is better to opt for clean-lined solutions such as blinds, shutters, plain fabric panels or

Right: Open stairs, where the treads are cantilevered from the wall, allow light through from area to area.

Below: A sunny upper landing, well lit with windows set into the slope of the roof, doubles up as a place for quiet reading.

curtains of pale, sheer material.

Slatted blinds made of wood or metal allow flexible light control; half-open they provide an element of privacy while evocatively striping the floor with moody bands of light and shade. Plain white fabric roller blinds are discreet and self-effacing. If you screen a window with a roller blind or fabric panel that extends right up to the ceiling and down to the floor, you can create the illusion that the window is larger than it is. Blinds can also be hung so they are pulled upwards rather than downwards, which allows you the option of only screening the lower portion of the window. Translucent shutters made of acrylic panels also

offer the opportunity to preserve one's privacy without blocking too much natural light.

VENTILATION

It is no accident that when people describe their experience of extremely confined surroundings they often say: 'It was so small I couldn't breathe.' Light, air and space are so profoundly connected that it is difficult to conceive one without the other.

Natural ventilation is not only vital for health, it also contributes to a sense of well-being. Modern office blocks, with their sealed windows and conditioned air, are deadened environments: the important thing about fresh air is that it is air on the move. Moving air creates a feeling of vitality and alertness; it also alters our perception of temperature. Most people can stand a higher degree of heat provided air is flowing freely – conversely, of course, it is the 'wind-chill' factor that makes cold days so bitter.

When you are living in a small space, it is essential that all windows should open fully to allow free passage of air throughout. Siting radiators underneath windows can aid the natural circulation of air within a space. In areas such as kitchens and bathrooms, where humidity can build up and odours linger, additional ventilation

may be required in the form of extractor systems. Chimneys, either open and ready to use or blocked off with an airbrick, also help to keep the air moving. Heat generating appliances such as tumble dryers should be sited in well-ventilated areas and may require external ducting.

LIGHTING SCHEMES
FOR SMALL SPACES

The way you light your home has an immense impact on both the way it feels and the way it works, yet few aspects of interior design are

often so poorly understood or so badly handled. One reason is that people concentrate too much on the appearance or style of light fittings, without pausing to consider either their effect or their positioning. Another is the perceived technical difficulty of the whole issue, which tends to lead to a reluctance to experiment. Yet another arises out of the notion of artificial light as a direct substitute for the real thing, which often results in rooms that are overlit by a single, bright central fitting, rather like a kind of indoor sun.

In any space, lighting can make all the difference between comfort and unease; in a small space that effect is heightened. And, since small spaces are often multipurpose ones as well, lighting has a particular role to play in defining areas of

Left: A strategically positioned skylight bathes a kitchen in natural light. A similar effect can be achieved by lighting a ceiling recess with concealed uplights.

Below and opposite: Light and colour make powerful allies, as demonstrated in this Philippe Starck-designed hotel, St Martins Lane in London. Guests can transform the mood of their room by changing the colour of the light at the touch of a button.

activity, enabling routine tasks to be performed safely and effectively without sacrificing mood and atmosphere. Light a small space badly and you will feel like you are trapped in a cell; light it well and you may not even notice it is small at all.

GENERAL PRINCIPLES

The basic principles of good lighting apply whatever the size of your home, but in a confined area the emphasis is on creating a sense of spaciousness, while at the same time providing a certain richness and variety of experience. The object is to avoid dull, uniform lighting that reveals all at once and kills atmosphere stone dead. There is nothing more depressing than a single light hanging forlornly from a central rose in the ceiling.

- Increase the number of light sources. Most homes are harshly overlit, but have too few light sources. If you increase the number of sources, each light does not have to be very bright for the general level of illumination to remain the same.
- Avoid central or high ceiling lights. Overhead lighting has a tendency to draw in the walls and make a space seem smaller. It is also bland light, illuminating all areas equally so that the effect is both dull and depressing. That said, a light hanging low over a dining table can work well.
- Reflect light off the planes of walls and ceilings to enhance the sense of volume. Uplighting a ceiling or the upper portions of walls increases the feeling of height; washing walls with light, from the side or floor level, generates a feeling of expansiveness.
- Avoid glare by concealing light sources. Glare occurs when there is too great a contrast between light and dark; it tires the eyes and causes a sense of unease.
- Create pools of light and shade to draw the eye through a space and define areas of interest. A number of lights positioned around the room at different heights can transform a single space into a series of related areas and thus create a sense of spatial variety.
- Graze surfaces and finishes with light. Lighting from the side reveals form and texture, adding an important element of richness where decorative treatments are otherwise subdued.
- Consider the effect of different light sources. Ordinary tungsten bulbs have a warm, yellowish glow which is inherently cosy and domestic. Halogen bulbs emit a much whiter and more sparkling light which enhances minimal contemporary styles of decoration. Avoid fluorescent light unless it is concealed behind a baffle that has a coloured interior to remove the harshness of this lighting.
- Use lighting as a means of creating spatial illusions. Shallow recesses or cutouts in ceilings can be invisibly uplit to suggest greater volume; extending light to outdoor areas carries views through from indoors to out.
- Provide a flexible lighting infrastructure. This means making sure there are enough power points so that wires do not trail everywhere and sockets are not overloaded, and fitting dimmer switches to enable light levels to be adjusted according to need and mood.

TYPES OF LIGHTING

Lighting can be broken down into categories, according to function. Most areas in the home will require a combination of different types.

- General or background lighting provides an overall level of illumination when natural light levels are low. This type of lighting can be supplied by table or floor lamps, uplights, downlights, spotlights and hanging lights.

Task lighting provides bright, focussed light for working areas. The classic task light is the anglepoise, with its adjustable arm enabling light to be directed wherever it is needed. Fixed lights, such as downlights, can provide task lighting for built-in worksurfaces.

Accent light makes a feature of decoration and display. Variations on the basic theme of the spotlight are the most common forms of accent lighting.

Decorative light is light for its own sake. The flickering flames of candles and fire, fairylights and sculptural objects that just happen to light up add warmth, wit and atmosphere.

LIVING AREAS

Enhance the sense of space with uplighting or spotlights directed at the walls and ceiling planes. Table and floor lamps beside seating areas create warm, intimate focal points; where seating is low, lamps of different heights can be used to provide welcome vertical emphasis.

Decorative displays, pictures or other points of interest can be picked out with small spotlights. It is generally best to avoid too much in the way of fixed lighting in living areas unless you are absolutely sure that you are never going to change the layout of the space or move furniture around in the future.

KITCHENS

Good task lighting is required for worksurfaces and other fixed points of the kitchen layout, which often means some form of fixed lighting arrangement, such as spotlights, track lights or recessed downlights. Downlights should be positioned to shine directly onto counters and worktops so that you are not working in your own shadow. A series of small pendants hung along the length of a counter will serve the same purpose; pendants with narrow cone-shaped shades focus the light effectively. Where the kitchen forms part of an open-plan space, make sure that task lighting is dimmable to shift the focus to living areas when the kitchen is not in use.

EATING AREAS

Pendant lights allow light to reflect off the surface of the table and draw people together in a cosy,

hospitable focus. If you have a pale-coloured tabletop or a pale cloth, light will reflect upward – the best light for dining as Vivien Leigh once told me! Several small pendants are often a better way of lighting a long table. Positioning is critical: too high and the light will cause glare for those sitting down, too low and the light will interfere with views across the table. Soft background lighting

Opposite: One of the abiding principles of successful lighting is to create pools of light and shade that draw the eye through a space. Avoid even levels of bright illumination, especially from a single overhead source.

Above and left: Fixed lighting, such as recessed downlights, are ideal for areas of the home where the layout is also fixed, such as kitchens and bathrooms. Lights concealed at the base of wall-hung units are another good way of illuminating countertops.

Right: Bedrooms call for flexible lighting. In addition to task lighting on each side of the bed for reading, gentle background lighting is also required, here provided by downlights positioned so that they do not shine directly in the eyes.

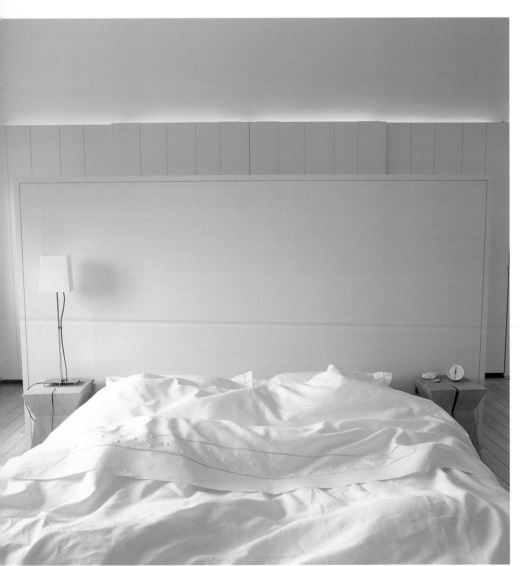

can be provided by table lamps on adjacent surfaces, floor lamps or wall-mounted uplights.

SLEEPING AREAS

Light both sides of the bed with table lamps, wall-mounted adjustable lights or small task lights. Avoid central overhead lights which can shine uncomfortably in your eyes when you are lying down. Make sure all lights can be controlled both at the entrance to the room and from the bedside to prevent yourself from having to stumble around in the dark. Where head height is limited, on a mezzanine level or sleeping platform, small uplights placed on the floor can help to counter any feeling of enclosure.

Left: Concealed lighting hidden at the top of a wall of fitted cupboards creates a soft background glow. A shaded table light at the bedside provides both decorative and task lighting for reading in bed. In sleeping areas, it is important to avoid the conventional arrangement of a central overhead fixture as it can be overly dominant when you are lying down. For optimum control, make sure lights can be switched on and off both from the entrance to the bedroom or sleeping area and from the bedside.

Right and far right:
Recessed downlights are ideal bathroom fittings. Special fully waterproof designs are essential. Water and electricity make dangerous companions, so it is advisable to check the suitability of any fitting before installation.

Below right: Robust recessed floor lights and halogen spots diffused by glass panels make practical yet atmospheric lighting for a bathroom.

BATHROOMS

Like kitchens, bathrooms are generally fairly fixed in layout, which means that fixed forms of ceiling light, such as recessed downlights, provide a good solution for general illumination. Light mirrors from both sides, not from the top, so that the face is evenly lit, without deep shadows. All bathroom fittings must be waterproof, with bulbs entirely encased and electrical connections fully recessed within walls or ceiling. This applies particularly in small bathrooms or wet rooms where the risk of water coming into contact with electricity is greater.

Right: Hallways and staircases need to be adequately lit for safety, but glaring, over-bright sources can be just as hazardous as lighting that is too low. The ideal is to create a soft, even background illumination using uplighters, wall lights or floor lights; downlights can also be effective in this context.

WORKING AREAS

Uplighting provides glare-free illumination for any work that involves computers and prevents distracting reflections on the screen. Other types of work – from drafting to reading to sewing – benefits from a dedicated task light that can be angled so that light falls directly on the focus of attention. Workbenches can be lit by fluorescent strips concealed behind wall-mounted baffles.

CIRCULATION SPACES

Halls, stairs and landings demand a good level of general illumination so that you can move safely from place to place – pools of light and shade which can be so evocative elsewhere in the home are less appropriate here and may cause you to miss your step. Nevertheless, if light is too bright or uniform it can undermine the potential drama of such transitional spaces. Omni-directional pendants can be strategically placed at intervals for a striking visual effect; downlighting is another standard solution. Wall-mounted uplights can be used to enhance volume in cramped spaces; individual floor lights recessed into the base of walls beside stairs or along corridors make a theatrical pathway.

Above: Fitted storage areas often benefit from fixed lighting, such as downlights, so that you can locate what you are looking for without fumbling around in conditions of semi-darkness.

Right: What is often termed 'information' lighting – the light inside the fridge or above the doorbell, for example – is generally fairly utilitarian. But as this external walkway demonstrates, more evocative effects can be achieved very simply. Here lights concealed behind a baffle emphasize the textural surface of brickwork while providing a lit pathway to the door.

case study
LONDON TERRACE CONVERSION

Opposite: Looking through the kitchen from the garden; the new internal window provides a connection with the living area at the front of the house. The cooking area is arranged along the length of one wall, with a line of base cabinets extending out into the garden. An external steel frame comprising a beam and post had to be extended beyond the building line to enable the glass door to slide completely open.

New views and vistas can transform one's experience of a space without necessarily increasing floor area. This adaptation of an existing rear extension dramatically opens out the entire ground floor of this small terrace house to create a seamless transition from the main living area at the front to the garden at the rear. The black granite worktop, which extends from the kitchen right out into the garden, underscores the clarity of the design.

To achieve this degree of openness, the internal walls on the ground floor were taken down from front to back. The kitchen area was created from two separate spaces and an internal window was made in the wall between the new open-plan living room and the kitchen to provide views through to the garden. At the back of the space, a sliding glass door meets a frameless glass panel, pursuing the theme of transparency; the door slides right away allowing the whole back of the house to be fully opened up to the outdoor space.

Material choices also have a part to play in enhancing the effect of natural light. Here, white paintwork and light-toned flooring indoors and out provide a clean, contemporary backdrop, while the black countertop serves as a graphic counterpoint, almost like a line on a drawing. Nothing else distracts the eye. Visual clutter, which contributes so much to the quality of a space, is relegated to high shelving and extensive kitchen cabinets below the counter.

Opposite: At the rear, a side window allows light to flood into the kitchen from two locations. The deep sill over the radiator is made of MDF painted black to match the marble worktop, while white walls and Portuguese limestone flooring – laid over underfloor heating – maximise the light potential of the space.

Left: The delicate leaves of bamboo planted beside the window create an animating shadowplay on the pale surfaces of the interior.

Right: The frameless glass panel, which provides a minimal separation between indoors and outdoors and an uninterrupted view along the worktop, is made of 12-millimetre-thick toughened glass. The edge of the glass engages with a groove in the sliding door in a neat piece of precision detailing.

The outdoor section of the worktop has an inset barbecue; cabinets beneath provide storage for dustbins and gas bottles. The outdoor cabinets are made of exterior quality MDF, specially painted for weather resistance.

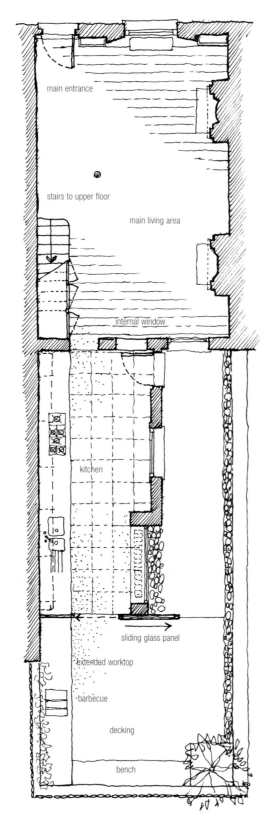

main entrance

stairs to upper floor

main living area

internal window

kitchen

sliding glass panel

extended worktop

barbecue

decking

bench

LONDON TERRACE CONVERSION 11 square metres

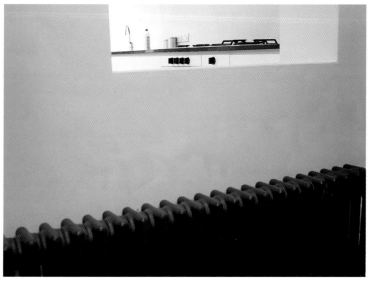

Left: The internal window between living and kitchen areas lets the light flow through from back to front.

Above: The seamless quality of the design owes much to the absence of extraneous fittings and fixtures. Ingenious detailing on the cabinets allows drawers and doors to be opened by means of finger gaps at the top. The cutout panel reveals a glass-fronted bar fridge for chilling drinks. The glass shelving above the worktop consists of a shallow trough of reinforced wired glass. Outdoors, the unadorned decking is made of narrow planks of tanalized (weather-treated) softwood.

case study
LONDON LOFT SPACE

Located within an old concrete-framed printworks converted for residential use, this loft-style apartment is actually quite small: only about 90 square metres. The plan of the space is also very deep, with windows only on the end wall. The main design challenge, therefore, was to make the most of available light and to retain as much of the feeling of scale and openness of the original industrial space as possible, while creating distinct areas within it to support different activities.

The solution was to create a raised platform down one side of the space and enclose sleeping and working areas using two sculptural 'blocks'. Cantilevered over the edge of the platform, the blocks appear to float in the space, leaving the original volume intact and readable as a single entity. Concealed up- and downlighting within the blocks accentuates this illusion. The decorative scheme, based around neutral-toned materials such as wood, brick, stone and metal, mediated with plenty of white, helps to make the most of both natural and artificial sources of light. Glass-topped tables create an unimpeded vista and also serve as light-reflective surfaces.

Successful open-plan living requires as much storage as possible. Both the blocks and the platform or plinth contain storage areas; further storage is provided by a built-in window seat and a storage wall in the entrance lobby. The result is a practical, flexible space that maximizes light and internal views.

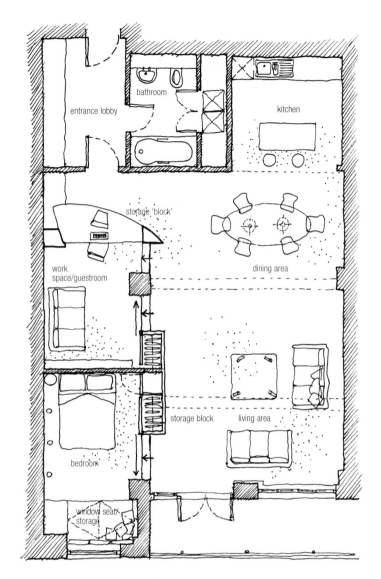

LONDON LOFT SPACE 90 square metres

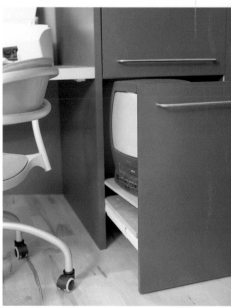

Right, top to bottom:

One wall of the guestroom is lined with shelving to store books and CDs; a sofabed provides overnight accommodation (top). The second of the two storage 'blocks' is in the form of a curve, which sweeps round to direct traffic at the entrance of the loft, coming to a sharp, prow shape at its apex. On the other side, the block houses a workstation, fitted with shelves and pull-out drawers tailor-made for specific storage requirements (centre and bottom).

Above: The kitchen area comprises a run of built-in units along the far wall and an island preparation counter/breakfast bar. White walls and fittings combined with well-positioned downlighting prevent this compact space from appearing cramped. Immediately adjacent is the dining area. The light, airy theme is continued here with a glass-topped dining table and white Jacobsen chairs. Two pendant lights above the table create atmospheric pools of light for evening entertaining. Flooring in the main living/dining space is light-coloured maple.

Above: In the main bedroom, a narrow internal window set into the top of the wall allows natural light to spill through to the adjacent guestroom while retaining privacy.

Above right: Uplights set into the floor enhance the sense of volume and supplement natural light.

Below right: Small wall-mounted halogen lamps on flexible arms provide directional light for reading on either side of the bed.

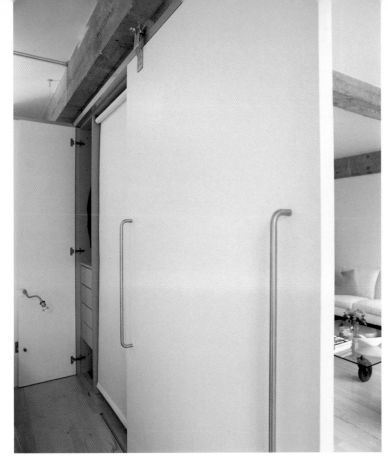

Top and top right: On the bedroom side of the storage block there is ample space for clothes storage. The industrial-scale sliding doors roll out on top wheels to provide full enclosure and privacy for sleeping; they are normally left open to allow light through from the main living area.

Above and right: A window seat built into the end wall of the main bedroom offers a comfortable, sun-drenched corner to relax in and yet more potential for storage.

case study
PARIS APARTMENT

Right: A mezzanine level built over the top of the kitchen area and bathroom provides a snug den for overnight guests.

Far right: Precision planning was required to fit all the appliances into the available space. Easy access to the fridge from the mezzanine shows just how tightly the space has been organized.

Below right: Steps up from the entrance lobby, which is now open to the rest of the space and defined by a half-height divider.

Living in small spaces often goes along with setting up home for the first time. Equally, however, it can accompany another shift in gear after the family has grown. At 36 square metres, this small Parisian apartment is only a third of the size of the owner's former home, a considerable downsize that required an entirely new way of thinking about space and belongings.

It's often easier to live with less when you haven't yet had the opportunity to acquire very much in the first place. In this case, the owner called upon an architect friend to help her make the most of the available space so that she could accommodate as many of her possessions as possible. Having lived in more spacious surroundings, the owner was initially wedded to the conventional arrangement of self-contained rooms. In particular, she wanted a separate dining room as the focus of the apartment. What the architect was able to demonstrate was that by opening up the space as much as possible and tailoring storage and built-in features for a precise fit, the number of possessions that were actually needed was much reduced.

The result fulfils the original brief, but in a much more fundamental way. The dining area, although not fully enclosed, serves as the hospitable heart of the apartment. By removing partitions around the double-height entrance, the space is flooded with natural light and imbued with a sense of calm: elemental qualities that are perhaps the most valuable possessions of all.

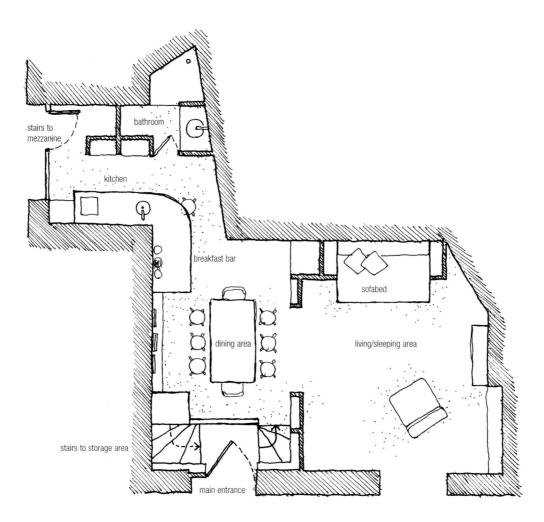

stairs to
mezzanine

bathroom

kitchen

breakfast bar

sofabed

dining area

living/sleeping area

stairs to storage area

main entrance

PARIS APARTMENT 36 square metres

Right: Neatly detailed built-in storage in the dining area accommodates table linen and cutlery for a clutter-free entertaining area.

Above: Open views through the apartment, from the living area, through the dining area and into the kitchen beyond. By removing doors and widening entrances, the sense of space and light was greatly enhanced.

Above right: The kitchen curves round the corner, ending in a breakfast bar that serves to connect the cooking area with the eating/serving area. Wrapping worksurfaces around corners exploits what would otherwise be wasted space.

Right: The open-plan arrangement of the space results in a logical flow of activities and allows light from the large front windows to penetrate all areas of the apartment.

Above left and centre: The view from the dining area focusses on the fireplace on the far wall of the living area. Superb materials add a quiet note of luxury. The flooring throughout is wide boards of oak, of the type used to make cognac barrels. The fireplace is simply detailed and lined in volcanic rock.

Left: View from the mezzanine level down into the dining area. Walls are plain polished plaster, waxed for a soft mid-sheen finish that reflects the light.

Above left: The tiny mezzanine sleeping area is minimally furnished with a futon. Every inch of space has to work for its living. A small bookshelf is neatly integrated above the bed.

Above right: Creature comforts: loose rugs and a television for cosy bedtime viewing.

Above: With the dining area as the main space for entertaining, the living area doubles up as a bedroom. The large comfortable sofa, covered with a velvet throw, pulls out and up to make a bed at night. A small basement area is devoted to a dressing area/wardrobe.

Above left: The wall behind the sofabed in the main living area is fitted with built-in storage to accommodate pillows and bedlinen right where they are needed.

colour, pattern & texture

The urge to decorate one's surroundings is very deep-rooted, arising from a basic human instinct for self-expression.

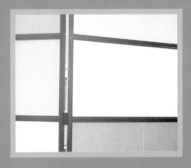

The urge to decorate one's surroundings is very deep-rooted, arising from a basic human instinct for self-expression. Evidence of this fundamental creative drive is present in all cultures, at all times throughout history; even where life seems a daily struggle, it is accompanied by the visceral thrill of colour or the satisfying repetition of pattern.

Different colours, patterns and textures have their own associations, both collective meanings that everyone shares and personal responses that connect with individual memories or tastes. Decoration is an important way in which such feelings are voiced, which is why it can have such a profound effect on your enjoyment of your home.

Superficially, small spaces may seem to impose certain limits on decorative possibilities. It is undoubtedly true that light and space – two sides of the same coin – are naturally emphasized by light, airy styles of decoration, while warm, rich colours and dense patterns tend to have the opposite effect of enclosure. Small spaces also require a greater degree of decorative uniformity throughout to keep visual distractions to a minimum, a sense of restraint that might appear to rule out richness and variety. The stock response to such apparent restrictions is the familiar modern palette of white walls, blond wood and pale surfaces and furnishings.

But decorating small spaces does not necessarily entail retreating down a neutral cul-

de-sac, nor is neutrality necessarily synonymous with the bland and insipid. Pure, spare and uncluttered schemes, if they are based around a sympathetic blend of materials, can have great depth of character. At the same time, colour and pattern have their own roles to play in small spaces, and often have a heightened impact by virtue of the fact that their use is more sparing.

When you are decorating small spaces it is particularly important to remember that colour, pattern and texture are rarely experienced independently of one another. This is most obvious when it comes to the choice of materials: a limestone floor, for example, may be a particular shade of light honey, but the colour is inextricable from its surface texture and any subtle patterning of the stone itself or the manner in which it is laid. Even if you are painting a wall, you are not simply adding colour – the same tone will look subtly different over brick, wood panelling or smooth plaster, or in matt, eggshell or gloss finishes.

Above: Schemes that are lacking in strong colour or bold pattern need not be insipid, provided they are rich in textural contrasts. In this conversion, the mellow tones of oak flooring, reclaimed from an old printers' workshop, add warmth and interest to the interior. The exposed brickwork walls, treated with masonry sealant to prevent dusting, provide a rugged, homely backdrop to clean-lined contemporary furniture.

Above right: The all white decorative scheme of the small bedroom overlooking the main living space has been kept deliberately clean and simple.

The universal appeal of decoration rests not merely in its capacity to add a sense of delight and pleasure to life; but also in its potential to transform spaces in a relatively instant and economical way. The instant approach to decoration – well-fuelled by television makeover programmes – can, however, obscure the longer term advantages of opting for good materials that last the course and improve with time. A coat of paint will freshen any space in a matter of hours, but solutions that are more than skin deep add an important sense of quality to the interior, a dimension that can go a long way towards offsetting any spatial shortcomings.

SPACE-ENHANCING DECORATION

There is a common tendency to conceive decorative schemes an area at a time. In some cases, there are practical reasons for this strategy – tackling one area at a time may well be necessary, for example, if you have to ration your time and expenditure. But there are certain risks in adopting this approach. The area-by-area strategy, as popularised by decorating magazines and programmes, effectively promotes the idea of the room as a blank canvas or stage set, awaiting the transforming magic of paint techniques and stylistic props. The consequence is that the interior becomes a convenient peg upon which to hang a succession of 'looks', with a bewildering variety of decorative styles from Moorish to Shaker coexisting under the same roof. Nothing is guaranteed to undermine a sense of space more.

In small spaces, particularly small multipurpose spaces, a piecemeal approach to decoration simply won't work. You need to consider the space as a whole and devise a

Above: The different surface qualities of materials introduce subtle variations in colour and texture. Warm, natural-wood kitchen units are given a sharper edge by the sleek stainless steel splashback, suspended shelving and metal detailing. Well-positioned downlighting further accentuates the difference in textures.

The decorative impact of the floor is often overlooked in this respect but its role, as one of the largest surfaces in any area, is critical. Extending the same flooring throughout a space, or restricting yourself to the same narrow tonal range in your choice of flooring materials, are tried and tested ways of enhancing the sense of space. For even greater impact, flooring materials that are the same in tone and similar in type can be used in adjacent outdoor areas so that boundaries are blurred.

As discussed in the previous chapter, a sense of space is often indivisible from a feeling of lightness and airiness, qualities that should also direct your decorative choices. White is undoubtedly the colour that makes the most of light, but there are an infinite number of subtle variations on the theme, ranging from natural neutrals to pale distancing tones. Again, the light-enhancing strategy works well outdoors. Painting

Above: White, natural and neutral tones are obvious space-enhancers. Many paint companies market a surprising number of different shades of white, from pure, chalky soft whites through to ivories and the palest cream.

Above right: An elegant, curvy partition divides sleeping and living areas.

scheme which provides a sense of unity and coherence from area to area, rather than abrupt transitions of style and effect. This is not to say that every space within your home must be treated in exactly the same way, but rather that there should be underlying themes that serve to tie it all together. Where spaces are interrelated or flexibly partitioned, or where there are internal views and vistas, that element of decorative consistency is all the more important.

Conceiving a scheme as a whole allows you to think in terms of planes that link areas together rather than a series of distinct spaces.

a facing garden wall white will serve to reflect light back into the interior. And, just as mirror multiplies the effect of natural or artificial light, reflective materials such as glass, perspex, polished stone or wood, steel or zinc surfaces and glazed tiles provide a lively or luminous quality that opens out one's perception of space.

DETAILING

Hand in hand with decorative simplicity goes simplicity of detailing. Although the word 'detail' seems to imply a certain degree of insignificance, in small spaces the cumulative effect of details can be very great indeed.

The most familiar types of detailing are traditional architectural and decorative flourishes, such as architraves round doors and windows, plasterwork mouldings, cornices, ceiling roses, picture and dado rails and skirting boards. Some of these features are pure embellishment; others combine decorative effect with practicality. The skirting board is a convenient means of trimming the base of a wall, a simpler way of achieving a straight, neat edge than plasterwork; similarly, cornices help conceal the type of superficial cracking that occurs at the right angle between plastered wall and ceiling. The original purpose of the dado rail was to protect wall finishes from being scraped by chair backs: in formally arranged eighteenth-century interiors, chairs were pushed back to the perimeter of the room when not in use. The purpose of the picture rail is self-evidently to serve as a means of hanging pictures.

Practicalities aside, such details serve also as proportional markers, part of the vocabulary employed by designers of previous centuries who adhered to the ancient traditions of Greece and Rome. Cornice, frieze and skirting board are

Above: Inside the curved partition (shown opposite) the architect has created just enough space for a tiny en-suite bathroom.

Below: A sympathetic blend of materials imbues a neutral scheme with vitality. Natural materials have an inbuilt harmony that is ideal for small space decorating. In a bedroom, tactile leather floor tiles are supremely luxurious underfoot.

essentially an interior form of entablature, dividing the plane of the wall according to the classical proportions of a temple façade. At the same time, such divisions came to signal the change between decorative treatments. The dado, for example, or area beneath the dado rail, was generally covered in a robust material, such as heavy wallpaper or panelling, contrasting with more delicate and refined finishes in the wall area above.

There are many things about minimalism that bore me but when it comes to the design of small spaces I would certainly go along with the minimalist approach to detailing – which is to do without it wherever possible. In small spaces fussy details are visual clutter, interrupting the planes of walls and ceilings unnecessarily. A flush door set seamlessly into a wall forms a continuous surface; a panelled door framed by an architrave calls attention to itself. Thorough-going minimalists take pains to do without skirting boards. Getting a straight edge at the base of a plastered wall presents something of a decorative challenge but

Above and centre: Simple, high-quality fixtures, such as the brushed steel door furniture and the curved bathroom tap, bring elegance to minimal interiors.

Opposite: Spaces look bigger when there is an absence of conventional trim, such as skirting boards, cornices and architraves.

is by no means impossible: one solution is to stop the plasterwork just short of the ground on a concealed beading so that the plane of the wall appears to hover over the floor – however, you'll have to be careful with your Dyson.

More prosaic details include the functional features of door handles and catches, knobs, switches and socket plates. Again, for the sake of clarity it is advisable to keep these as discreet as possible or to do without them altogether. I have recently changed the brass switch and plug points and the white china door handles in my house to metal knobs and plates, which has made a significant difference. Sliding doors or panels need only shallow depressions to serve as fingergrips; cupboards can be fitted with press catches so that they swing open at a touch; the tops of drawers can be angled so they can be pulled out without the need for knobs or handles. If a kitchen area within an open-plan space is conventionally detailed, you can never get away from the sense that you are sitting in the kitchen. On the other hand, if it has a seamless, streamlined quality it can become almost as self-effacing as a white wall when not in use.

USING COLOUR

Colour is a powerful decorative tool. In small spaces it can be harnessed both to emphasise light and views and to provide an accenting element of vitality.

In broad terms, light colours, or those that contain a great deal of white, reflect most light and therefore increase the sense of space. Dark colours, on the other hand, absorb light to a greater degree and thus generate a feeling of enclosure. A similar distinction can be made between 'warm' and 'cool' colours. For various

Top: Blocks of strong colour, repeated in kitchen units and upholstery, breathe life into an otherwise muted scheme for an open-plan space.

Above: Edgy colours such as blue-grey are very successful in small spaces. These cool tones are naturally distancing, which helps to increase the sense of space. Using the same colour in different applications creates a subtle thread to draw a scheme together.

scientific reasons to do with the way we see light, warm colours, such as yellows, reds and oranges, appear to 'advance', which means that a red object, for example, will look closer than it actually is. Cool colours such as blues, greys and violets, by contrast, serve to distance objects in space. The obvious application of such characteristics in decoration is to exploit the distancing effect of cool shades to create the illusion of pushing back the walls.

At the same time, consideration must also be given to conditions of natural light. In warm, south-facing areas, the palest shade of blue-grey will appear incredibly fresh and spacious, but in darker, north-facing areas the same colour will simply be chilly and dreary. Where natural light levels are low, a neutral shade with a hint of warmth – a creamy white, for example – will reflect light and provide a more comfortable and hospitable backdrop.

WHITER SHADES OF PALE

White and all the near-shades of white are obvious choices when it comes to decorating small spaces. In fact, they are obvious choices full stop, particularly for those who find it difficult to

take the plunge and opt for stronger, brighter shades. Many people who are shy of using colour assume that by adopting a neutral scheme they cannot go far wrong. The risk, however, is that neutral decorative schemes can be bland and dull. Success often rests on slight variations of tone – there might not be all that much difference between pure white and magnolia, for instance, but whereas white is fresh and invigorating in the right circumstances, magnolia almost always saps the life out of a room.

White rooms are somewhat of a contemporary cliché, firmly associated with the 'less is more' philosophy of minimalism. Stark and perhaps a little too pure to be human, this spare modernist aesthetic is generally assumed to have derived from the work of Le Corbusier. In fact, many of Le Corbusier's most influential schemes reveal an evocative interplay of colour and texture.

If you look back at earlier uses of white in the interior, however, it is clear that white can have somewhat richer connotations. One of the first to advocate white as an interior finish was William Morris, who appreciated the integrity of plain whitewash, not merely as a utilitarian finish but as a backdrop 'on which light and shadow play so pleasantly'. While such a notion of painting fine rooms white was shocking in the extreme for Morris's Victorian contemporaries, by the end of the nineteenth century the idea had gained favour in progressive and artistic circles. White played a role in the aesthetic of 'sweetness and light' that defined the Edwardian country house; more influentially, it also became synonymous with a kind of heightened sensitivity. The all-white interiors designed by Charles Rennie Mackintosh were charged with a sense of soft enveloping intimacy. Several decades later,

society decorators Elsie de Wolfe and Syrie Maugham layered white on white to create interiors of chic, brittle luxury.

As such examples reveal, much depends on the precise nature of the white you choose and the way in which you handle it. Matt, chalky white – similar to the old pre-war distemper or Morris's whitewash – has a down-to-earth honesty which works well in combination with natural materials and rugged textured finishes. The sensual, luminous effect of the mid-sheen ivory in Mackintosh interiors is accentuated by the use of white painted woodwork and pale carpeting. Glossier whites are enhanced by other highly reflective surfaces, such as glass and mirror. In any situation, an all-white scheme calls for careful matching: off-white will simply look discoloured next to pure white.

Tinting white with the merest suspicion of colour can result in agreeably edgy shades, such as pale lavender or blue-grey, colours that hover on the cusp of warm and cool. These tones inject a little more vitality into an essentially neutral decorative scheme and have the added advantage of heightening the colour of almost any strong accent used in combination with them. A similar effect can be achieved by applying a very thin colourwash or glaze over a pure white background. Venture a tone or two darker, however, and you are into pastel territory. Pastels, a sort of 'colour lite' for those too scared of the real thing, run the real risk of looking twee and fainthearted.

BACKGROUND & FOREGROUND

If small spaces call for light, airy backgrounds, this does not mean that you have to foreswear the use of strong colour altogether.

Opposite and right: Planes of strong colour can be used in an almost abstract fashion to define space, a strategy that is particularly effective in open-plan areas. Alcoves, end walls and doors are all surfaces that are ideal for this approach.

Above and opposite:

Reminiscent of the house built by Charles and Ray Eames in California in 1949, this bedroom enclosure consists of a steel framework infilled with panels of perspex and coloured paper.

Interconnecting spaces, where walls, ceilings and floors are treated as continuous planes, can be interrupted by blocks of colour to signal a change of activity; if surrounded by plenty of white, those colours can be fairly intense without compromising the sense of space in the slightest. Using colour in this fashion helps to dissolve the conventional notion of the 'room'.

A sophisticated version of colour coordination can also be used to great effect in a small space. At its most banal, coordination tends to mean those safe and expected decorative schemes where the colours of walls, soft furnishings and decorative detail are all variations on the same basic shade, and the result is all too often a deadening of atmosphere and mood. If, however, you repeat a colour in small doses from area to area – so that the blue-grey of the kitchen units crops up again in the colour of bathroom tiling or in the throw draped over a sofa – you set up a thread of connection that links areas together in a subtle fashion and creates an inbuilt sense of harmony.

Perhaps the simplest way of adding the vitality of colour to a small space is to use it as an accent. Even such minor details as pictures, vases of flowers, throws, cushions and rugs can contribute substantial jolts of colour that are all the more welcome for the reticence of the background. The added bonus of such a strategy is that such accents are easy to change, which all helps to keep the interior full of life and vitality.

USING PATTERN

Pattern introduces a sense of movement to the interior. There is something about repetitive designs that people seem to find inherently comfortable and reassuring. Psychological

Above: Nothing adds a greater depth of character to an interior than materials that have stood the test of time. This Thames barge, lovingly renovated, features original oak alongside new timbers replacing those damaged by water. The kitchen counter is also made of oak.

studies of perception have found that the human mind particularly enjoys patterns that are orderly and symmetrical.

Superficially, pattern may seem to have little role to play in the decoration of small spaces. In conventional terms, pattern is often synonymous with a type of visual busyness or a desire for romanticism – the countrified prettiness of rose-patterned wallpaper and chintz, or the exotic layering of Eastern rugs and textiles – but there are many other types of design that work well in small spaces and serve to add that important rhythmic dimension. Geometric patterns – such as plaids, checks, stripes or spots – are particularly compatible with small space decoration.

We also tend to think of pattern as a feature of fabric – designs that are woven, printed or applied. But if you broaden the concept it is apparent that there are other ways of exploiting pattern in the interior. The way tiles are laid on the floor or wall makes a pattern of a sort; slatted blinds are every bit as striped as a striped fabric; herringbone or basket-weave parquet are patterns that echo those in woven or plaited materials. These pattern nuances add an essential liveliness when colour is restrained and surfaces are otherwise plain.

Like colour, pattern can be used in a remedial way to adjust scale and proportion. Wooden strip flooring laid so that the direction of the boards runs from the front of a room to the back will increase its apparent length. Curtains with a vertical stripe will accentuate the height of a window. In some cases, it can be a question of matching the scale of the repeated element with the proportion of the area. The tight grid that results from using small tiles or mosaic suits confined spaces, such as bathrooms.

Pattern can also be introduced in the form of a decorative accent. Fractals or photographic blow-ups can provide an alternative to a block or plane of colour as a way of defining an area of activity. Rugs and carpets – from kelims to striped dhurries to contemporary art rugs – also offer the opportunity to anchor a seating arrangement within an open-plan space.

USING TEXTURE

Where pattern stops and texture begins is not clear cut. Both are inherent in material quality. Natural materials – such as polished stone or scrubbed oak – have great depth of character and improve with age and use. Sleek manufactured materials – such as stainless steel, acrylic and glass – introduce a contemporary edge.

Texture is one of the most important decorative elements in small spaces. Where you have to restrict yourself to a fairly narrow palette of colours and where the opportunities to ring the changes with pattern are also somewhat limited, textural contrast supplies the necessary degree of visual variety. Different surfaces reflect light in different ways: a polypropylene chair may be exactly the same shade of white as one made of wickerwork, but they will appear subtly distinct from one another.

The appeal of texture is not merely visual. Texture implies touch – the feel of the soft nap of a blanket against the cheek, the sleekness of a metal balustrade under the fingers, the smoothness of bare floorboards under bare feet. Things that are pleasant to touch add sensuality to everyday experience; they also provide a sense of comfort and security. A common way that people derive comfort from their surroundings is to fill their homes with belongings and the

Right: The built-in bed was custom made from iroko, a West African hardwood with a rich colour, and incorporates extensive storage underneath, as well as a radiator.

Above: Ceramic tile, mirror and, unusually, a basin made of hardwood create a discreet interplay of textures and surfaces in a bathroom.

Above right: Tilework has an inherent sense of liveliness due to the repetitive grid in which it is laid or applied. Light grey mosaic tiling is set off by pristine white grout.

cosiness of clutter. In a small area, where such an approach would inevitably compromise any spatial quality, textural contrast can supply a similar sense of ease and delight.

The contrast of textures relates to the way we experience the natural world. During a coastal walk, for example, you might expect to encounter different types of terrain – firm, compact sand at the water's edge, dry, sifting sand beneath the dunes, rocky outcrops and springy turf along the clifftops. Such changes, from smooth to soft, rough to resilient, are part of the pleasure of being outdoors. One might compare this with the deadening experience of walking a similar distance across an expanse of level asphalt. Changes of texture in the interior provide subtle

Right: A slatted wooden floor adds a softening touch to a bathroom clad in hard, reflective materials. Texture is all about touch – a dimension that is often overlooked in decorative schemes.

Left: A striking example of the effectiveness of reflection, this mirrored bathroom wall literally doubles the perceived amount of space. Slate wall and floor tiles create a moody, sensual background.

shifts of gear, often barely perceptible but essential to keep interiors full of vitality.

The closer the contact, the more textural quality matters. Choose thick, soft towels and bathmats, fine linen or Egyptian cotton sheets, duvet covers and pillowcases – all fabrics that are a delight to touch. In living areas, the warm weight of wool throws and blankets, feather-filled cushions covered in velvet or brocade, crisp, heavy-duty cotton covers on sofas and armchairs banish the sensory deprivation of artificial fibres.

Textural contrast can also translate into practical material choices. Different areas in the home often call for different conditions underfoot – comfort where you sleep, easy maintenance where you cook the supper. If you keep to the same basic light tone but vary the flooring materials you can maintain spaciousness while addressing the practicalities. For example, light ceramic tiles might define a kitchen area, with hardwood used as the main flooring for a living space and pale jute carpeting a bedroom.

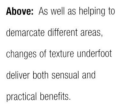

Above: As well as helping to demarcate different areas, changes of texture underfoot deliver both sensual and practical benefits.

Top: Textural quality is particularly important next to the skin. This cedarwood tub rings the changes on the more expected porcelain or enamelled bath. Wooden tubs must be expertly crafted or they may leak.

Above: Beechwood veneer wall panels provide a warm and sound-proofed enclosure for a bed. The two recesses house downlights.

case study
LONDON GARDEN FLAT

Opposite: The private entrance to the apartment is via the garden, which also serves as a place for entertaining in fine weather. The decking is made of wide iroko boards; the table, in iroko and stainless steel, is the architect's design. The insulated glass doors providing access from the apartment fold right back, and a lightweight aluminium and canvas canopy pulls out to extend the living area outdoors.

Converted by an architect for his own use, this tiny flat on the ground floor of a Victorian house in London has a total floor area of only 28 square metres, but clever detailing, logical planning and a luxurious use of materials have resulted in a clean-lined, flexible space full of depth and character. While white walls and pale floors are a common decorative strategy for small spaces, the rich tones and graphic material contrasts displayed in this apartment strike a note of contemporary sophistication.

A principal aim was to link interior and exterior spaces more closely and to provide a sense of overall clarity in the design. All original mouldings were removed and a wall that formerly divided the kitchen from the living space was taken down. New windows and large folding glass doors leading into the garden were installed. With the new kitchen area occupying the length of one wall and extensive storage built in along the opposite wall, the centre of the space was dramatically opened up.

Textured stone-effect wallpaper and flooring made of solid oiled walnut create an enveloping mellow background. An Eastern influence, evident in the sliding screen that divides the bedroom from the main living area, also extends to the design and landscaping of the garden: the outdoor space is planted with Japanese maples and ornamental grasses set against the contrasting textures of solid iroko decking, concrete paving and a ceramic fountain.

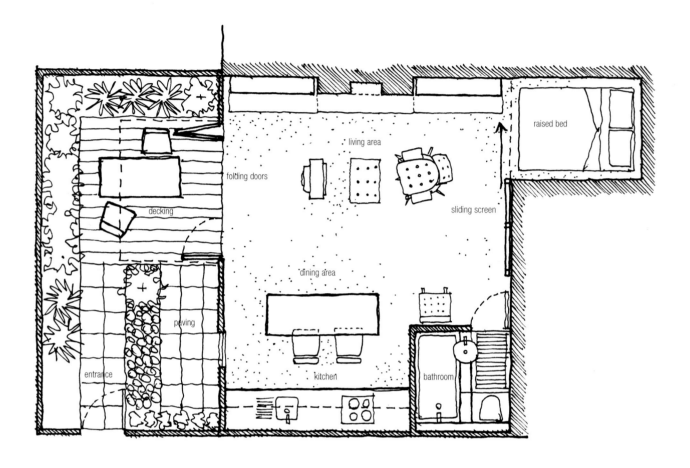

raised bed

living area

folding doors

sliding screen

decking

dining area

paving

entrance

kitchen

bathroom

LONDON GARDEN FLAT 28 square metres

Right: A polished marron marble counter and splashback provide a graphic counterpoint to the warm bleached sycamore used on cupboard doors. The dining table, specially designed for the space, doubles up as an additional kitchen worksurface.

Above: The wall in the living space is fully fitted with storage cupboards for CDs, books and clothes. The fireplace, which has been raised, has a gas and ceramic log fire and a marron marble hearth. The cupboards are faced in brushed aluminium, with solid bleached maple tops. Cantilevered glass shelves run the length of the alcoves to either side of the chimney breast.

Left: The kitchen cabinets are designed to house all necessary appliances and equipment including water softener, fridge-freezer, washer-dryer, mini-dishwasher, microwave, boiler and a handy flip-out ironing board.

Left: At only 1.5 square metres the bathroom design called for a high degree of ingenuity to accommodate all the fittings. The door, made of double-layered mirror and sandblasted glass, serves as a giant reflector, throwing the light in the bathroom back into the living space. The bathroom itself is fully waterproof. A solid iroko duct board has an enamelled shower tray underneath. The marron marble vanity counter has a tap that can be swivelled from basin to bath.

Right: The aluminium clad cupboards in the living area have a soft reflective sheen, enhanced by judicious positioning of directional downlights.

Above and right: The bed is raised up over a built-in wardrobe and fits snugly into the space. The screen that partitions off the sleeping area is made of ebonized oak, aluminium and paper twine; behind are two ebonized sliding doors that provide access to the wardrobe. Instead of a ladder or fixed steps, access to the bed is by stepping on a side table and from there onto the built-in wall cabinet, both of which have been specially reinforced to take the weight.

case study
PARIS STUDIO

Years ago, this tiny studio was literally a monastic cell, providing basic accommodation within a building that once housed a religious community. Very few of the original features remain, except for the main door and fireplace. But what is striking about the place is its sense of volume. Although the floor area is a mere 30 square metres, the height is a very generous three metres, lofty proportions that generate a feeling of expansiveness.

When the architect owners decided to convert the space, they were determined to maintain its airy, open quality. Their solution was to group all the essential amenities of the flat – from the bed to the kitchen and study area – within one timber-framed construction occupying most of one wall. Working out the details of all the fitted elements was like piecing together a jigsaw, a process underscored by the strong colours used to pick out different surfaces and planes. With the timber structure faced in a warm sycamore veneer, the complementary palette of orange, yellow and red serves to link the existing structure with the new.

Integrating cooking facilities, storage and a sleeping area within close proximity to one another meant that extra care had to be taken with servicing. Cabling and pipes run under the floor, sheathed in concrete channels; an extractor hood keeps cooking smells at bay and the joists that support the sleeping platform are wrapped in wool to cut down on noise and vibration.

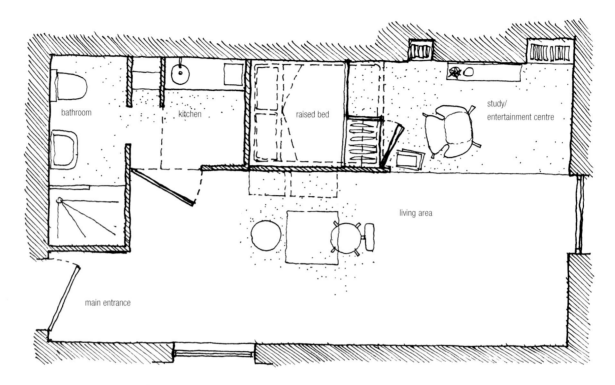

bathroom

kitchen

raised bed

study/
entertainment centre

living area

main entrance

PARIS STUDIO 30 square metres

Right: The kitchen is extremely simple, comprising a stainless steel worksurface, hob and sink, with a vividly coloured ventilation hood over the top.

Far right: The TV is built in behind a perspex panel. Above is a cubbyhole for the CD player. The flap-down desk screens a computer.

Right: The high ceiling meant that a sleeping platform could be comfortably accommodated, leaving enough head height for access. Underneath is hanging space for clothes storage. The ladder that provides access to the platform is not fixed, but is stored in a cupboard.

Far left: A strong blue picks out a dividing wall which serves as a combined bedhead and nighttable and makes a vibrant contrast to the scarlet bedlinen.

Left: The marble fireplace is one of the few original features, providing a graphic counterpoint to bright, contemporary furniture.

organization

The central dilemma of living in a small space can best be summed up by a single word: stuff.

The central dilemma of living in a small space can best be summed up by a single word: stuff. It's not so much what we do at home as what we keep there that causes the problem. Possessions always seem to arrive with a one-way ticket: they come into our lives and then rarely depart. And they do accumulate – not only those belongings that are proof of your own passions and preferences, but things you just seem to acquire somehow along the way.

Minimalists would remind us that 'less is more', but I'm afraid a real strain of dishonesty often runs through those apparently spare and pure interiors. Minimalists are just as fanatic about possessions as everyone else, the only difference is that they hide their things behind cupboard

doors. In Japan, where the Zen philosophy of 'thinglessness' originates, there is a similar paradox. The Japanese are the most gift-giving culture in the world; they are also exceptionally keen on acquiring the latest in technological wizardry. The result is that many Japanese interiors are evidence of a two-way tug between the desire for spatial serenity and the need to house burgeoning amounts of clutter.

There is no getting away from the fact that clutter and small space living are simply not compatible. To live in a small space with any real chance of comfort, you have to exercise a certain degree of discipline. It helps if you are naturally neat in the first place and if you don't rate shopping as your favourite form of relaxation.

But the real key is not an iron-willed determination to resist any form of purchase or a ruthless approach to the sock drawer: it is simplicity. Simplicity means doing without the superfluous, so that you surround yourself with belongings that really serve their purpose. It also means systems of organization that are natural and easy to use.

CLEARING OUT

The very first step towards good organization is to clear out redundant clutter. Years ago, I was standing in my former shop in Manhattan when a rather wild-looking woman came in and proceeded to tear round the store, gathering up huge quantities of different storage items. 'When I woke up today I decided to get organized!' she proclaimed. I couldn't help but think that, by adding more clutter to what she already had, she was going at the problem the wrong way round.

Clearing out should be easy but, of course, it isn't. I was a war child, brought up in times of exceptional austerity, and as a consequence I absolutely detest waste and find it very difficult to throw things away. At the same time, I find light, airy, open spaces immensely uplifting, so something has to give.

You don't have to have lived through the war to find it hard to get rid of things. Hoarding is an instinctive response to any form of threat or insecurity, a psychological hedge against the possibility of future deprivation. In our materialistic society, acquiring more and more consumer goods is also seen as good thing in itself; we use our possessions as a way of defining ourselves and our position with respect to other people. But many of us simply derive immense comfort from owning things, things that trigger chains of thought or enshrine certain memories.

There comes a point, however, when things start getting the upper hand. Things breed things: you need things to look after things, things to keep things in, things to go with other things. You don't have to live in a small space to suffer from the effects of escalating clutter, it is merely that if your space is limited you will reach saturation point rather sooner than someone who has a spare room or attic to dump it all in.

Clutter devours physical space. If you only wear one-third of your wardrobe, that represents a direct loss of two-thirds of your clothes storage space. If half of your filing cabinet is filled with paper that could be thrown away, half of the drawers might as well not be there. Getting rid of clutter liberates the space it formerly occupied, which is the most basic spatial equation of all.

Clutter can be wasteful in other senses, too. The more belongings you have, the more time you will have to spend looking after them. And looking for them. When every drawer and cupboard is stuffed to the gills, the chances of laying your hand on something when you want it are remote, which is why many people end up owning items in duplicate and triplicate.

While I am rather amused by the notion of clutter consultants, who perform the service of 'dejunking' on behalf of other people, I acknowledge that the whole process of sifting through your belongings can arouse uncomfortable feelings. A constant niggling concern is whether or not you will regret the decision to get rid of something sometime in the future; then there is the fear that you will upset people if you don't hang on to the presents they gave you; added to which is perhaps an element of guilt at how much money you've spent on clothes that don't fit or suit you, sports equipment you never use or books you haven't read or will never read again. Clutter consultants are in business chiefly because it can be very difficult to untie these emotional knots yourself.

Once the knots are untied, however, the experience can be immensely cathartic. Holding on to things keeps one foot permanently in the

Below: You can keep a surprising number of possessions in a room without compromising the sense of space provided you treat storage in a wholehearted, almost architectural fashion. This working wall of bookshelves organizes a complete library, but reads as a single entity.

past; letting things go can impel you in fresh, new directions. I've recently undertaken a massive clear-out at my house in the country and I was struck by the degree to which the whole process literally stirred up the atmosphere. That sense of exhilaration was a considerable help at those moments of indecision when I stood poised between returning something to a shelf or drawer and consigning it to the wastepaper basket.

Opposite: Concealed storage is fairly essential if space is limited, particularly for everyday necessities that may not contribute very much visually. Here a wall of fitted shelves is screened by simple Japanese-style sliding panels made of ricepaper framed in wood.

WHAT TO DISCARD

The most useful way to decide whether or not to keep something is to apply William Morris's oft-quoted golden rule: 'Have nothing in your houses that you do not know to be useful or believe to be beautiful.' While the qualities of usefulness and beauty are to some extent subjective, the things that fall into the following categories are likely to be taking up space without contributing anything positive to your life:

● Things that make you feel guilty. Unwanted gifts are an obvious source of guilt, so are items of clothing that no longer fit or never suited you in the first place, books that you have never got round to reading, and any purchase made on impulse and regretted the second you left the shop. It is amazing how quickly the guilt can evaporate once the object that inspires it has gone from your life.

● Things that are worn out, that have been broken for a long time or that you have replaced with a newer model. I am a firm believer in the virtue of thrift and would much rather take an old pair of shoes to the mender's than buy a new pair. But nowadays it is also important to accept that, with the pace of technological change, a certain degree of wastefulness is built into the process of consumption. If something has been broken for a long time, chances are the parts will no longer be available to repair it. And, if you have managed without it for a while, chances are that you don't really need it.

● Things that you rarely use. Here you need to distinguish between those things one can only use at infrequent intervals – such as Christmas decorations – and the things you don't use as often as you imagined you would when you bought them. Everyone goes through short-lived enthusiasms, whether it is for ice skating or ice-cream making. When those enthusiasms fade, it is time to dispense with the equipment that goes along with them. Kitchen gadgets often fall into this category. When your kitchen space is limited, everything in it should earn its keep. It's often better to have a free worksurface than a machine that takes up a lot of room in exchange for performing a routine task a second or two faster than doing it by hand.

● Things that you are saving for a rainy day. Many people are gripped by an odd compulsiveness to collect items of small practical value – carrier bags, for example, or string. This is all well and good if you reuse what you save, but not if the act of saving threatens to turn into hoarding. One family who were clearing out the home of an elderly relative discovered a number of boxes into which string had been sorted according to length. One box, full of tiny pieces, was labelled 'String Too Small To Keep'. I'm all for eccentricity, but perhaps that goes too far.

● Paper trails that lead nowhere. The old adage that if you keep something in your in-tray for long enough, events will take over and you will no longer have to deal with it applies to much paperwork. Candidates for the out-tray include old accounts; receipts, guarantees and instruction manuals relating to equipment you no longer own; back copies of magazines, brochures and old newspapers.

Spring cleaning should apply to every season, but it is as well to accept that even a major clear-out will keep you ahead of the game only so long. With practice you may find you can bring the same critical awareness to bear at a much earlier point in the process, before you even make a purchase. Ask yourself: do I want it?

Above: This platform bed provides scope for a great deal of built-in storage underneath: pull-out hanging rails and shelving accommodate clothes and even the steps up to the high-level bed have been designed in the form of modular storage cubes.

Do I need it? Will I use it? And, finally, where will I put it?

STORAGE SYSTEMS

Once you have freed your life from redundant clutter, the next step is to organize what remains in an accessible and orderly way. Both aspects are important: for organization to smooth your path, it must be tailored to the way you perform everyday tasks and routines.

Accessibility means evaluating your belongings according to a kind of hierarchy of use. On the face of it, it may appear common sense to group your belongings so that you store all your kitchen equipment in the kitchen, for example, or all your clothing in a designated closet or wardrobe. But it often makes for a better use of space to decant those items that are necessarily used only infrequently or seasonally and keep them elsewhere, away from the main areas of activity. Large platters and roasting tins that only see service at Christmas could be put away with the Christmas decorations – the small effort of retrieving them once a year is worth the extra space in your kitchen cupboards the rest of the time. You might also consider rotating your wardrobe so that winter clothing gets packed away during the summer months. Accounts and files you need to keep for statuatory purposes or for future reference need not occupy valuable filing space in your day-to-day work area.

Orderliness is of paramount importance in a small space. In practice, this means keeping floors as clear as possible and building in fitted systems of storage. You can house a surprising amount of your possessions in working walls of shelves and built-in cupboards without compromising the sense of space; start piling things up on the floor, however, and that quality will be quickly eroded. Fitted storage enables you to work within the existing architectural framework and create a seamless, clutter-free look. Traditional free-standing storage, in the form of wardrobes, dressers, chests of drawers and so on, has a tendency to eat into floor space and makes room layouts and circulation routes unnecessarily awkward.

Predictably, Le Corbusier was a great advocate of fitted storage, recommending 'built-in fittings to take the place of much of the furniture, which is expensive to buy, takes up too much room and needs looking after'. His point of reference for storage was the 'Innovation' trunk, which had a compact, fitted interior that displayed the same functionalism as the modern aeroplanes and automobiles he so admired. In a similar way, borrowing ideas from industrial or commercial contexts – such as office filing cabinets, trolleys, robust metal shelving and shop rails – can provide added flexibility to small space storage.

Fitted storage rooms or areas may appear, at first glance, to represent an indulgent waste of space when you do not have much area at your disposal. But by condensing clutter and confining it to a designated area, this strategy can make

Left: Storage needs are particularly acute in kitchen areas where a wide variety of foodstuffs, utensils and equipment must be kept close at hand. As elsewhere in the home, there is often a tendency for cupboards to silt up with clutter; regular reviews of what you keep and why can be a good space-saving strategy.

Above: Bench seating in a dining area incorporates storage space underneath.

the rest of your home much more workable.

An obvious example is the separate dressing area. Building in cupboards and hanging space in a vestibule or connecting area between a bedroom and bathroom demands the sacrifice of only a few feet of floor area, but the benefits to adjoining spaces can be immense. In the same way, running fitting cupboards or drawers the entire length of a wall provides a neat and integrated solution for housing a wide range of everyday items.

The best systems of organization allow a certain degree of latitude for growth and change. Uncrowded bookshelves, drawers that are not filled to the brim, closets that aren't bursting at the seams contribute just as much to a sense of spaciousness as other more obvious factors. Storage should not place you in a mental straitjacket so that everything must be immediately returned to its proper home the minute you have finished with it. To feel comfortable in your surroundings, you need the option of making a mess from time to time.

Below left: Tailor-made shelving for an extensive vinyl and CD collection.

Below, centre and right: Borrowing a shelving system used in libraries, these metal units on castors double up for twice the storage space.

Shelving is the ideal way to store many different types of possessions, including books, CDs, videos, kitchen supplies, files and reference materials – all categories of objects that can be grouped and stood upright, folded or stacked. While banks of open shelving do have a somewhat busy look, you can mitigate against any excessive feeling of enclosure by making sure there is plenty of surrounding breathing space. With open shelves, at least you can see where things are at a glance.

Shelving is best conceived wholeheartedly, so that it occupies the whole of a wall or an entire alcove from top to bottom. This has much more coherence than isolated groups of shelves placed indeterminately around the room. Like any other form of fitted storage, it is essential to tailor the dimensions of shelves to what you propose to store on them. You can calculate the length of shelving you need by measuring your books, records and so on; at the same time, be sure to take into account the different heights of your belongings so that shelves can be spaced the appropriate distance apart. Larger, heavier or taller items look more visually comfortable arranged on lower shelves, where they are also easier to access. Narrow shelves may be appropriate for small items that can get pushed to the back and overlooked; glasses, for example, are best stored no more than two deep and the same is true of foodstuffs such as herbs and spices that you need to be able to retrieve quickly. It is also important to be generous with the amount of shelving that you provide so that there is room for expansion. Shelves that are crammed with items create an uneasy sense of overload.

Detailing and construction should be as discreet and self-effacing as possible. Painting shelves in with the main wall colour is less obtrusive; shelving over a kitchen counter can be made of safety glass for a light, minimal look. Shelves that are cantilvered out from the wall using invisible or concealed shelf supports are

Right: Where storage meets display: Ron Arad's 'Bookworm', a snaking curve of metal shelving, displays its full potential in the designer's own home.

Above: One solution to the problem of finding somewhere to put the bike: suspended from the ceiling by a rope and pulleys.

elegant solutions in situations where you only want a single shelf or where shelving is to be widely spaced.

In practical terms, the most important consideration is making sure that the means of fixing, material, span and thickness of shelves are adequate to bear the loads you will place on them. Solid masonry walls support greater weights than partition walls; brackets or vertical tracks should be securely screwed and plugged into position. Thicker shelves can span greater distances without buckling or sagging. Of the manufactured woods, MDF is particularly dimensionally stable. You can trim the leading edge of shelves with a deep moulding to increase the appearance of solidity and provide additional bracing. You may think that there is a great advantage in having adjustable shelving, but I have yet to meet anyone who has actually altered the position of their adjustable shelves once they have put them up.

HANGING STORAGE

Another basic way to keep floors clear is to hang things up. At the simplest, hanging storage can consist of nothing more elaborate than a version of the Shaker peg-board. The Shakers hung up everything from brooms to chairs, an approach that reflects the fact that they viewed possessions as practical tools, designed for specific purposes and not for show: you used what you needed and then you hung it up again.

Hanging storage is ideal for things you need to keep close at hand, within easy reach. In the kitchen, wall racks and rails make a convenient place to suspend utensils, pots and pans and other items of the *batterie de cuisine* that you use on a daily basis. Coats, hats, jackets and other outdoor wear are easier to retrieve from a series of coat hooks lined up along the length of a wall than from a coat stand where everything has a tendency to get jumbled up together. Bicycles can be hung from robust wall brackets so they do not create an obstacle in a hallway. You can also fit narrow rails or hooks to the backs of cupboard doors to organise flattish items, such as towels, ties and scarves or saucepan lids.

In a small space, however, hanging storage can looked cluttered in itself, no matter how orderly the arrangement. Belongings that are kept out in the open also have a tendency to get dirty and dusty unless they are in regular use. Clothes, in particular, benefit from concealed systems of storage where they will not fade in direct light. Aside from woollens and jerseys that stretch and small items of clothing such as underwear, many articles of clothing are best organized by hanging. The optimum arrangement is to double-hang the bulk of your wardrobe, so that two rails are fitted one above the other. This makes particular sense if you have only a limited area, such as an alcove, in which to house your wardrobe. Hanging storage can be concealed by simple flush doors painted in with the main wall colour or by blinds or paper screens. Sliding doors or panels that do not open outwards are more space-saving.

CONTAINMENT

Organizing things in boxes, drawers or other forms of container has a certain fundamental appeal; part of the pleasure of possession seems to be bound up with the satisfaction of tucking our belongings away in secure places. (Freud had something to say on the subject.) Containers provide dual practical benefits: they allow like to be housed with like, and they hide a vast amount

Right: Bicycles may be
beautifully engineered but
they take up a great deal of
space. Parking them in the
hallway only creates an
irritating obstacle. Here a pair
of bikes are held upright,
where they take on an
almost sculptural quality.

of clutter from view. They can also be nested, providing a means of subdividing categories of belongings – the cutlery tray that fits inside a drawer is an obvious example.

Storage boxes are available in a wide range of materials, from stout cardboard to plastic, canvas and leather, and in uniform or graduated sizes. A neat array of containers and file boxes can transform a working area from jumbled disorder to a model of discreet efficiency or provide a valuable means of stowing away videos, tapes and CDs which might otherwise prove too visually distracting in a living area. Simple chests and file drawers serve a similar purpose.

Containers also allow you to exploit out-of-the-way corners as storage areas. Shallow-lidded boxes on castors can be slid under the bed and used to store shoes, linen or out-of-season jumpers in dust-free conditions. Units with pull-out baskets or drawers can accommodate sports equipment or household accessories in the area beneath the stairs.

It is important to bear in mind, however, that the whole notion of containment can be taken too far. Pocketed shoe tidies and drawer dividers that sort pants and socks individually often add a vexacious level of extra work to what should be a simple and user-friendly means of organization. At the opposite end of the extreme, slinging a load of unrelated objects into a drawer or box, where they will languish out of sight and out of mind, is not much of a storage solution either.

MODULAR STORAGE

Fitted kitchen units and free-standing storage systems that can be assembled in various configurations provide an element of visual continuity in hard-working areas where storage is a

Above and right: Children and good organization are not natural companions, but providing places to keep their belongings in order is a start. This ingenious unit flaps down to reveal a hanging rail for clothes storage and extra surfaces for creative play.

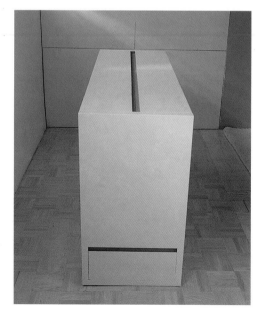

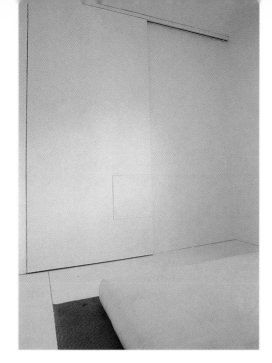

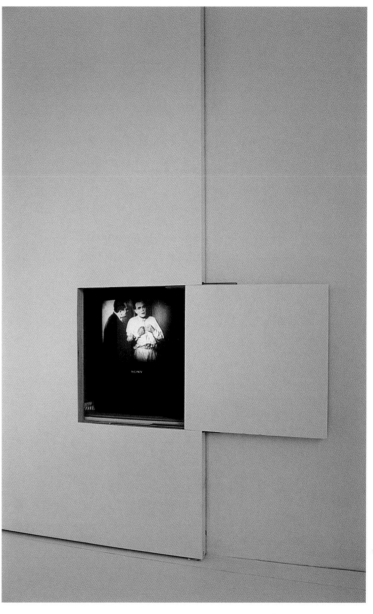

Top: If you really can't stand having any of your possessions on view, you can always opt for total concealment behind discreet white panels.

Above, left and right: A full-height panel slides across for access to a wardrobe, while an inset panel can be slid across independently for watching television in bed.

Below: The area underneath the bed provides a useful place to keep a variety of items, from shoes to bulky jumpers and bedlinen. This design takes the notion a stage further, incorporating deep drawers below the bed and fitted cupboards and shelving as a surrounding framework.

Below right: The higher the bed, the more room for storage underneath.

priority. Such systems tend to be produced in basic modules – 600 millimetres, for example, is the standard width of a fitted kitchen unit – which means an element of customization may be required to make full use of the space they offer. Interior shelves that can be fitted at different heights and pull-out trays and baskets provide flexibility.

At the lower end of the market, fitted kitchen units and wardrobes can have a rather cheap and nasty aesthetic. One solution is to make use of the basic carcass and upgrade with better doors and drawer fronts, fixings and handles. The same approach makes an economical way of updating existing fitted kitchen or clothes storage.

Built-in units can have a heavy, boxy look that dominates a small space. A simply remedy is to do without the coverstrip or plinth at the base so that the supporting legs are revealed and the units

seem to hover slightly over the floor. Alternatively, set the plinth back some distance to avoid dirt accumulating underneath.

SIMPLICITY AND FUNCTION

I am a particular fan of the work of Heath Robinson, whose cartoons characteristically feature delightfully dotty contraptions that take the idea of functionalism and labour-saving to absurd extremes. One of my favourites, 'How to Live in a Flat', shows a couple sitting at a table, 'served' by a complex system of wires, pulleys and levers, a neat satire on middle-class anxieties when confronted by the necessity of living in a small space. In Heath Robinson's cartoons, ingeniuty always goes a little bit too far.

Years ago, I was tempted in that direction myself when I was living in a small flat. To gain extra space, I decided to suspend a table from the ceiling so that it could be raised up on pulleys when not in use. Unfortunately, however, eating off that table was like eating off a swing and I had

Above left and right:
Complete kitchens in a single unit are now produced by some manufacturers, ready for slotting into place. Comprising sink, hob, cooker, ventilation hood, and storage, and with folding screens to hide it all from view, these 'kitchens in a box' are models of tight ergonomic planning.

Left and below: Spaces don't come much smaller than this. The bed is tucked into a wedge-shaped corner immediately adjacent to a basin, which is concealed under a pull-up top, and immediately above a cupboard housing a washing machine.

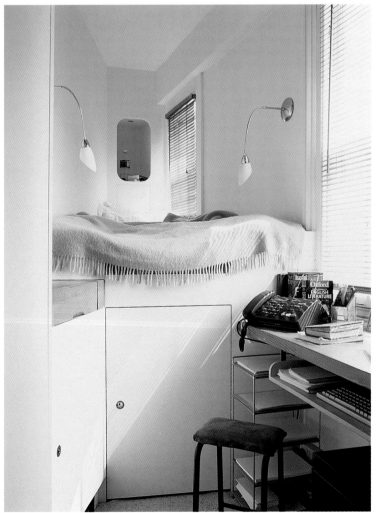

Above and top: Today, foldaway, or 'Murphy', beds are robust and well-designed – no sudden surprises! to build a plinth for it to rest on, which rather defeated the point of the exercise. The whole situation was rather reminiscent of that staple joke of old comedies – the foldaway bed that always folds away at inopportune moments, trapping its unwary occupant in a cupboard.

Small space living undoubtedly calls for a degree of ingenuity, but that ingenuity must genuinely work. Neat space-saving ideas are often based around elements that fold down or slide out: the ironing board that pulls out from a kitchen counter or flaps down from a cupboard, the table that can be extended by adding in extra leaves, the bench seat fixed to the wall that can be folded back when not in use. Modern foldaway beds pose little risk of accidental entrapment, with their counterbalanced spring mechanisms and secure wall anchorage.

Ingenuity can also take the form of multipurpose furniture and fittings. In recent years, designers have increasingly focussed on 'transformable' furniture, pieces that challenge the conventional furniture stereotypes, just as open-plan living challenges the traditional concept of the room. Tom Dixon's 'Jack' light – a light you can sit on or a seat that lights up – is a case in point. Transformable 'sofatables' or beds-in-boxes that can be used for sleeping, storage or seating are other examples. There is a slight risk, however, with furniture and fittings marketed as 'multipurpose' that none of the purposes are particularly well served. A cheap sofabed, for example, is often not very comfortable for either sitting or sleeping; better, but equally space-saving solutions might well be to buy a sofa of decent quality and a futon or rollaway mattress that can be stored out of the way when not in use – or buy a comfortable bed that can be accessorized with cushions during the daytime to form a seating area.

Real multipurpose value can often be gained by focussing on simplicity. You don't need separate services for tea and coffee when

Centre: Multipurpose furniture is an area of increasing design experiment. This 'sofatable' by Huzefa Mongan with its box cushions that double up as seats has an appealing simplicity.

Left: Like a clever piece of origami, this 'table=chest' by Tomoko Azumi folds out into a coffee table or stacks to make a bedside or occasional table, complete with drawers.

all-purpose mugs will do. Ovenproof dishes and casseroles obviate the need for separate serving dishes. A plain table works just as well as a desk or a dining table; simple folding chairs provide perches for eating, working or extra seating indoors or out. Upholstered floor cushions can be stacked for comfortable lounging or laid out to create a floor-level mattress. Stools are portable seats, occasional tables and bedside repositories for books and task lights. Modular seating units that can be moved around to create different layouts provide inbuilt flexibility and avoid the dominating statement of the sofa. A common response to the problems of furnishing a small space is to attempt to create a facsimile of a larger space, but reduced in scale, a strategy

Opposite: The raised floor of a kitchen and dining area incorporates deep drawers in the base for extra storage. The success of such features relies on seamless detailing.

Below: Few people have the luxury of a 'spare' room these days but accommodating overnight guests is a particular problem if you live in a small space. This bed base is fitted with a large drawer to house a spare mattress.

Below right: For the Imelda Marcoses of this world, whose shoe collections are threatening to take over: pop-up floor-level storage takes the shoe tidy into a whole new dimension.

Above: Where storage meets display: good-looking basics, such as china and table linen, need not be hidden from view. Displays of everyday things create an easy-going and hospitable atmosphere.

Above right: A brilliant blue panel – actually a painted artist's canvas – slides across to conceal the fireplace and the inevitable television. Audio-visual equipment can be particularly intrusive in a small space.

Right: Deep ledges support a collection of framed photographs, which achieve greater impact displayed as a group than they would dotted around the room.

that can result in an uncomfortable sense of living in a doll's house. Simple, adaptable furnishings, on the other hand, maintain the quality of space without compromising function or comfort to any degree.

One area where miniaturization really does work is in the field of technology. There is no longer any need for a working area to be dominated by a huge computer terminal now that laptops have become so powerful; giant speakers and amplifiers are no longer required to enjoy the sound quality of a concert hall. Flat-screen televisions may soon cause the disappearance of the 'box' from our living rooms. The programmable home, with digitally controlled alarm systems, heating, lighting and music is no longer the stuff of science fiction. While such sophisticated technological infrastructure remains expensive and subject to breakdowns, the improvement in the quality of space may well be worth the extra investment.

DISPLAY

What makes a place feel like home are those belongings that we treasure for their own sake. Small space living inevitably entails focussing on function and doing without superfluous objects or detail, but that does not mean you have to live in a monastic cell. While pictures, flowers, photographs and mementoes may not be household necessities, they feed the human spirit.

Many minimalist ideas can usefully be adopted in the design of small spaces. Where I part company from minimalists, however, is in their absolute insistence on bare walls and empty space. For me, there comes a point where 'less is less'. In an empty room devoid of any features whatsoever, absolutely anything that happens to

Above: Living in a small space does not mean banishing all signs of life from view. Grouping decorative objects or pictures so that they read as a whole, and leaving plenty of breathing space in between, enables small apartments to look cosy but uncluttered.

If you have many treasured possessions, you might consider circulating the objects you choose to display. Changing what you put on view keeps interiors alive and full of vitality.

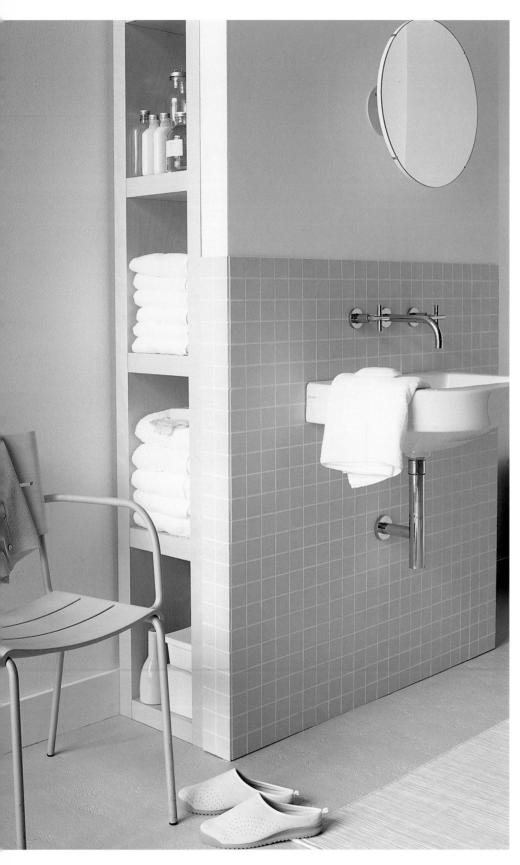

be lying about becomes an attention-grabber of the first order, which is all very well when it is a piece of fine art but less inspiring when it is a toothbrush or a duster.

In a small space, some kind of balance must be struck between the soothing nature of uncluttered space and those details that serve to animate it with a human presence. Le Corbusier recommended keeping all one's pictures in a cupboard so that they could be brought out and

Left: Pulling a wall forward slightly creates space for a neat array of narrow open shelving on the side. Such well-considered solutions combine practicality with aesthetic appeal.

Above: A redundant doorway has been transformed into a handy shelved recess to provide extra storage for attractive tableware.

Above and left: A free-standing shelving unit provides essential storage and divides a home office area from an open-plan living space. The semi-transparent and opaque panels of different colours allow some light from the window to filter through maintaining a sense of openness and adding an attractive element to the interior.

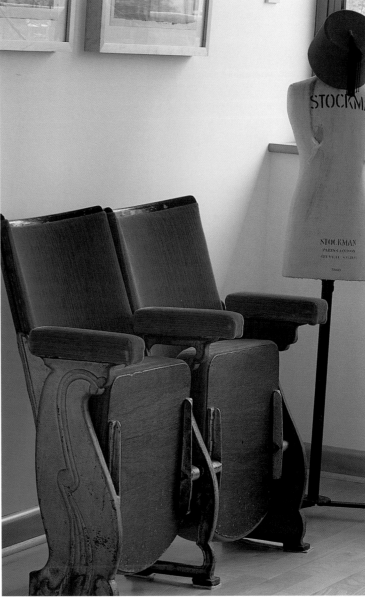

Above and opposite: Small should not mean purely functional: there's always room for the animating presence of whatever moves you – beautiful ceramics, a pair of old cinema seats or pebbles brought back from a stroll on the beach…

displayed one at a time. A similar notion can be found in the traditional Japanese house, where the space set aside for the purposes of serene contemplation typically includes only a low table, a vase in a niche or a pot of chrysanthemums.

This is not to say that you should only display one thing at a time, merely that scattering lots of things around the walls and on tabletops will make a space seem small no matter how cleverly it is

otherwise designed. The answer is to create a display area where objects or pictures are grouped and to leave other walls and surfaces bare to provide breathing space.

Display is all about vitality and appreciation. But if you stare at the same picture for years on end, you simply stop seeing it. In small spaces, changing what you place on view from time to time breathes new life into your surroundings.

Opposite: A larder cupboard
provides storage for basic
provisions. When everything
is concealed, storage must
be carefully planned. Here,
the MDF cupboards are made
with concealed hinges and
magnetic touch latches.

case study
LONDON LOFT SPACE

Nothing compromises a sense of space more than the presence of everyday clutter. Possessions may occupy no more actual area when they are stored in open view than when they are concealed, but the resulting visual busyness can still make the walls appear to close in. Small space living demands a certain degree of discipline, both in terms of tidiness and in terms of resisting the temptations to accumulate clutter. In this case, the clients were naturally unacquisitive and preferred a rather ascetic lifestyle. Their loft-style apartment takes the strategy of concealment to the ultimate. All belongings, from books and CDs to clothes and food, are hidden from view, along with kitchen appliances, socket plates and audio-visual equipment. What remains is simply pure space, full of light and calm.

With a floor area of around 92 square metres, this apartment in a converted match factory is not a true loft in terms of scale. The design brief was to maximize the dimensions of the space, while at the same time accommodating all the necessary features of modern living. Rather than compartmentalize the space with partitions, which would have produced a layout similar to a conventional flat, storage, services and other fitted elements have been built in, largely down the length of one wall. Even the lavatory is located in a cupboard. Ceiling height was sufficient to raise the sleeping area up on a deck, with a home office slotted in below.

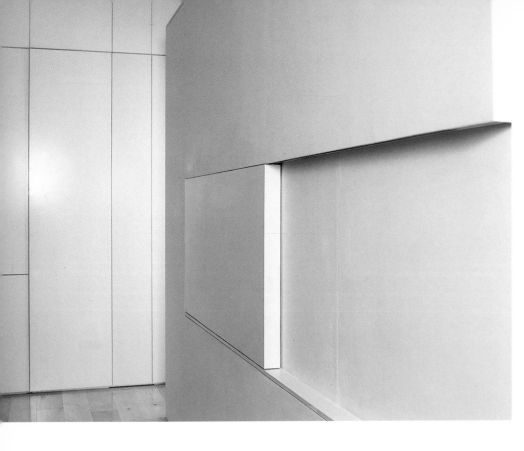

Left: A sliding panel hides the home office from view. All the MDF surfaces were spray-lacquered for a smooth, mid-sheen finish. Flooring is birch-faced laminate. Because there is underfloor heating, laminate was chosen over solid wood because it is more dimensionally stable.

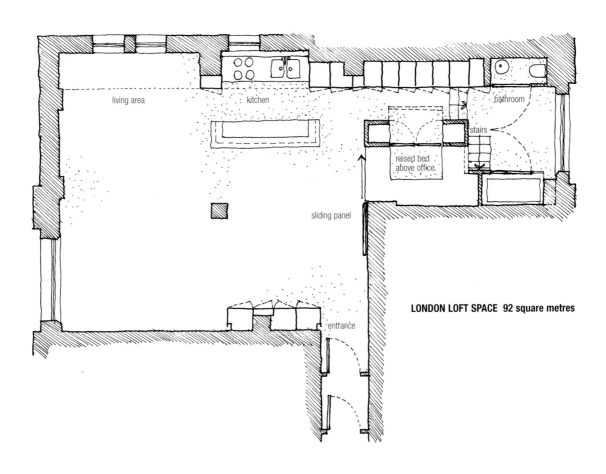

living area

kitchen

bathroom

stairs

raised bed above office.

sliding panel

entrance

LONDON LOFT SPACE 92 square metres

Above: View of the home office with the panel slid back. At the rear are the stairs to the bed deck. The deck consists of the bed itself and a walkway providing access, which is raised up at a slightly higher level to give headroom in the office area.

Right: Detail of the kitchen area. Sink, hob and fridge are slotted into a recess on the wall side. In front is an island unit that accommodates an oven, more cupboards and a dishwasher. An etched glass panel diffuses light from a window behind the hob.

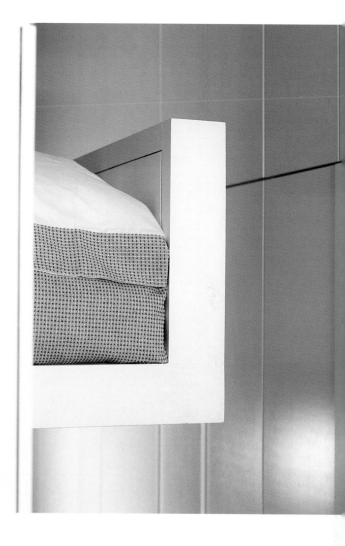

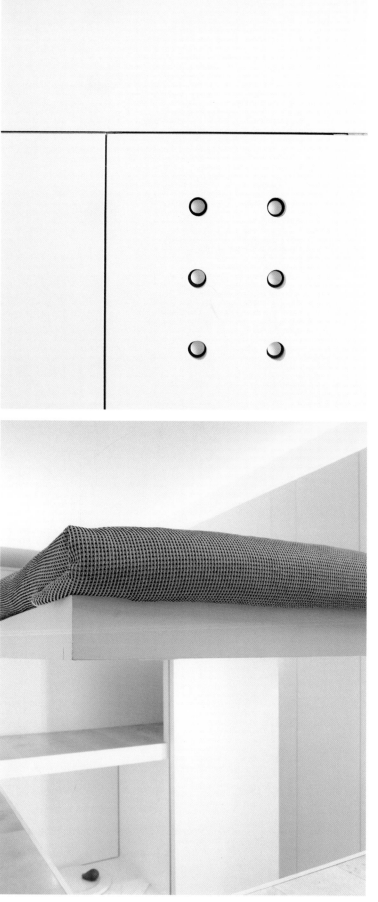

Opposite: Detail of the stairs up to the bed deck. Lack of conventional detailing, such as mouldings and trim, gives clarity to the space.

Above: Light switches are grouped at key positions in the apartment rather than dotted around from place to place. Conventional wall plates are simply concealed behind panels, with cutouts for the actual switches. Many of the cupboards incorporate uplights to accentuate the volume of space.

Left and above: The bed is surrounded by a walkway and cantilevered from a raised platform so there is no need for legs. The construction is in timber.

case study
NEW YORK WORK SPACE

Right: The wooden structure in the 'home' position. Extending from the structure is a low cushioned bench that acts as a sofa and guest bed. When the cabinet is opened to the 'work' position, the cantilevered sofa automatically glides away to be concealed behind the opened panels.

Working from home imposes additional demands on any space, but when there is a limited amount of floor area the problem is even more acute. In this small one-bedroom apartment in New York, the challenge was to design a space that functioned both as a home and an office. The client, a graphic designer who works at home full-time, required not only work space but somewhere that looked professional enough on the occasions when his clients visited.

The apartment is only 55 square metres, not big enough for a whole room to be devoted to an office. The ingenious solution was to create a transformable space that separated the two functions completely, so that during the working day the apartment served as an office and during the evening and weekend it truly felt like a home. This was achieved by means of a folding wooden cabinet that allows the client to convert the living space into an office space, and back again, on a daily basis.

Complex design thinking was required in order for the structure to be operated smoothly; the result is a successful contemporary version of the old 'fitted room' idea. The free-standing structure replaces a wall that used to divide the living area and bedroom. In the 'home' position, the structure is solid on all sides and all materials associated with work are completely hidden from view. In the 'work' position, it opens to offer two complete work stations.

Above: Large bi-folding doors swing open to reveal two complete work stations. The structure is made of maple ply and is operated by a ceiling-mounted steel track system. Smooth, effortless functioning is essential for an operation carried out on a daily basis. Although the result appears simple, detailing was very complex.

NEW YORK WORK SPACE 55 square metres

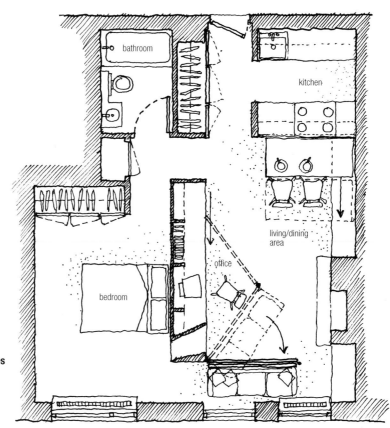

Above: The open panel in the structure frames the window in the living room with its views of the Hudson River. A key consideration of the design was to avoid blocking light. The other panel turns inwards to provide a hanging board for displaying work.

Left: View of the living/dining area. The dining table is on wheels and can be glided into position to serve as an additional worksurface.

Above and above right: When the structure is open or closed, a deep opening at one end provides a 'false perspective' window that allows light and views through from the bedroom to the living/work area and vice versa. The structure was designed to hover just below the ceiling so that it does not read as a solid wall.

Right: On the bedroom side, the structure doubles up as a tall headboard, complete with flap-down nighttable and fixed lighting.

index

acknowledgements

The publisher would like to thank the following photographers, agencies and architects for their kind permission to reproduce the photographs in this book:

Front Cover: Verne Fotografie; Back Cover: Peter Aprahamian/Living Etc/ipc Media; **2** Dan Holmberg/Photonica; **7** Paul Warchol (Architect: LOT/EK); **8 left** Robert Schoen/Still Pictures; **8 right** Mads Mogensen (Architect: Anders Landstrom); **9 left** Richard Felber; **9 right** Verne Fotografie; **10 left** Paul Chesley/Gettyone Stone; **10 right** Michel Arnaud/Judy Casey Inc.; **11** Andreas Pauly/Open Office; **12 left** Michel Arnaud/Judy Casey Inc.; **12 right** Nicolas Tosi/Stylist: Catherine Ardouin/Marie Claire Maison; **13 above** Designer: Douglas Ball; **13 below** Mark Wagner/Gettyone Stone; **14 above** Dave Young; **14 above centre** Dave Young; **14 centre below & below** Nicholas Tosi/Stylist: Catherine Ardouin/Marie Claire Maison; **15** Ford Motor Company; **16** Simon Brown/The Interior Archive; **17** Rodney Weidland/Belle/Arcaid; **18-19** Pear Tree (Treehouse) Ltd; **20 above** Paul Warchol (Architect: Lee Harris Pomeroy Associates); **20 centre & below** Christoph Kircherer/Stylist: M.Kalt/Marie Claire Maison; **21** Paul Warchol (Architect: Lee Harris Pomeroy Associates); **22** Mads Mogensen (Architect: Anders Landstrom); **24-25** Chris Gascoigne/View (Wells Mackereth Architects); **27** Debbie Treloar/Homes & Gardens/ipc Media (Architect: Jonathan Clark); **28** Richard Powers (Architect: Garry Marshall); **29** Peter Aprahamian/Living Etc/ipc Media (Architect: Nico Rench); **30** Richard Powers (Architect: Robert Dye Associates); **31 above** Giorgio Possenti/Vega MG; **31 below** Richard Felber; **32 left** James Morris/Axiom Photographic Agency (Architect: AH MM); **32 above right** Paddy Eckersly (Formwork Architects); **32 below right** Nick Carter; **33** Ian Parry/Abode; **34 above & below** Craig Fraser/Stylist: Shelley Street; **35** Peter Aprahamian/Living Etc/ipc Media (Architect: Nico Rench); **36 above left** Winfried Heinze/Red Cover (Architect: Gough-Willets); **36 above right** Hotze Eisma/Production: Rianne Landstra/Taverne Agency; **36 below** Marianne Majerus (Architect: Barbara Weiss); **37** Richard Powers; **38-39** Christian Sarramon (Architect: Gae Aulenti); **41** Mads Mogensen

(Architect: Marco Constanzi); **44-45** Nick Carter; **47** Paul Ryan/international interiors (Designer: Felix Bonnier); **48-49** Solvi Dos Santos; **52-57** Louise Bobbé/Elle Decoration (Architect: Burd Haward Marston; **58-63** Gracia Branco/Iketrade (Architect: Stefano Coro); **64-69** Jonathan Pile/Tonkin Architects; **71** Alberto Piovano/Arcaid (Architect: P.Robbrecht); **73** Andrew Bordwin; **75** Richard Glover (Arthur Collin Architect); **76** Alberto Piovano/Arcaid (Architect: P.Robbrecht); **77 above left & right** MINH + WASS; **77 below left, centre & right** Richard Waite/Arcaid (Moutard Architect); **79** Verne Fotografie; **80 above** Jan Verlinde (Designer: Francis D'Haene); **80 below** Verne Fotografie(Designer: Francis D'Haene); **81 above left** Andrew Wood/The Interior Archive (Designer: Kate Blee); **81 above right** Ed Reeve/Living Etc/ipc Media; **81 below** Petrina Tinslay/Arcaid (Designer: Valerie Harvey); **82** Nicholas Tosi/Maison Madame Figaro; **83** Richard Bryant/Arcaid (D'Soto Architects); **84** Alberto Piovano/Arcaid (Architect: Kris Mys); **85 left** Peter Aprahamian/Living Etc/ipc Media; **85 right** Studio-Azzurro Milan (Project: Cutini-Ossino); **86** Jonathan Pile (Architect: Project Orange); **87 above & below** Guy Obijn; **88 above left & right** Richard Bryant/Arcaid (Architect: Seth Stein); **88 below left** Richard Powers/Arcaid (Architect: Margery Craig & Associates); **88 below right** Richard Powers (Architect: Margery Craig & Associates); **96-101** Jean-Francois Jaussaud; **105** Richard Glover (Ben Mather Architects); **106** Jan Verlinde (Architect: Ponette); **107** Robin Mathews/Homes & Garden/ipc Media (Architect: Jonathan Freegard); **108 above & below** Richard Powers (Architect: Buschow Henley) **109** Edina van der Wyck/The Interior Archive (Designer: Victoria O'Brian); **110-111** Stephen Inggs/Stylist: Shelley Street; **112 above** Verne Fotografie (Architect: Johan Laethem); **112 below** Ray Main/Mainstream (Architect: Martin Lee Associates); **113 left** Ray Main/Mainstream (Sergison Bates Architects); **113 right** Chris Gascoigne/View (Architect: Alan Powers); **115 above left** Guy Obijn (Architect: Carlo Seminck); **115 above right** Nick Carter; **115 below** Peter Aprahamian/Living etc/ipc Media; **116** Ray Main/Mainstream (Sergison Bates Architects); **117 above** Ed Reeve/The Interior Archive; **117 below** Tim Beddow/The Interior

Archive (Architect: Garrett O Hagan); **118 left** Winfried Heinze/Red Cover (Architect: Tom Pike); **118 right** Eric Morin/Stylist: D.Rozenszroch /Marie Claire Maison; **119** Andreas von Einsiedel; **121** Nick Carter; **122** David Churchill/Arcaid (Architect: Stickland Coombe); **123 above** Richard Glover/View (Reading & West Architects); **123 below** Ed Reeve/ The Interior Archive; **124 above left & right** Eduardo Munoz/The Interior Archive; **124 below** Jan Verlinde (Claire Bataille & Paul Ibens Design for Obumex); **125 left** Chris Gascoigne/View (Simon Conder Architects); **125 above right** Chris Gascoigne/View (John Kerr); **125 below right** Chris Gascoigne/ View (Wells Mackereth Architects); **126** Nick Carter; **127 left** Chris Everard/Elle Decoration; **127 right** Jonathan Pile (Architect: Project Orange); **141 left** Eric Morin (Architect: Sylvie Bouron); **147** MINH + WASS; **149** Chris Everard/Elle Decoration (Theis & Khan Architects); **150 left & right** Peter Aprahamian/Living Etc/ipc Media (Mathew Priestman Architects); **151** Dominic Blackmore/Domain (Wells Mackereth Architects); **152-153 above** Christoph Kicherer (Architects: Briffa Phillips); **153 below** Richard Powers/Elle Decoration (Architect: Buschow Henley); **154 left** Nick Hufton/View (Anelius Design); **154 right** Gilles de Chabaneix/ Stylist: M.Kalt/Marie Claire Maison; **155** Jonathan Pile (Architect: Project Orange); **156 above** Andrew Wood/The Interior Archive (Architect: Tonkin Architects); **156 below** Peter Cook/View; **157** Dennis Gilbert/View (Conran Design Group); **158** Robert Dye Associates; **159** Winfried Heinze/Red Cover (Architect: Gough-Willets); **160-161** MINH + WASS; **162-163** Sheva Fruitman; **164 left** Richard Glover/ View (Reading & West Architects); **165** E.Barbe/Stylist: F.Sportes/ Marie Claire Maison; **166** Peter Aprahamian; **167 left** Chris Gascoigne/ View (John Kerr); **167 above right** Chris Gascoigne/View (Simon Conder Associates); **167 below right** Debi Treloar/Homes & Gardens/ ipc Media (Architect:Jonathan Clark); **169-173** Interior and Product Designer: Mark Humphrey; **175-177** Vincent Leroux/Stylist: Gael Reyre/Marie Claire Maison (Architect: Guillaume Terver); **179** Clive Frost (Designer: Ron Arad); **181** Chris Everard/Elle Decoration (Theis & Khan Architects); **183** Richard Glover (Arthur Collin Architect); **185** Ray Main/Mainstream (Architect: Chris Cowper); **186** Chris Tubbs/

Red Cover; **188 left** Chris Tubbs/Living Etc/ipc Media; **188 centre & right** Ed Reeve/The Interior Archive (Architect: Adjaye & Associates); Clive Frost (Designer: Ron Arad); **190** Holze Eisma/Production: Rianne Landstra/Taverne Agency; **191** Chris Tubbs/Living Etc/ipc Media; **192-193** Eduardo Munoz/The Interior Archive (Architect: Picado/De Blas); **194 left** Solvi Dos Santos; **194 right** Thomas Stewart/Living Etc/ipc Media (Architect:Mooarc); **195 above left & right** Richard Powers (Fulham Kitchens); **195 below left & right** Peter Aprahamian/ Living Etc/ipc Media (Architect:Urban Salon); **196 above right, centre & below right** Luke McCarthy (Designer: Huzefa Mongan); **196 above left & below left** Ed Reeve/The Interior Archive (Architect: Adjaye & Associates; **197 above, centre, below** Thomas Dobbie/ Designer: Tomoko Azumi; **198** Peter Aprahamian/ Living Etc/ipc Media (Architect: Nico Rench); **199 left** Richard Powers (Architect: Buschow Henley); **199 right** Circus Architects; **200 above right** Thomas Stewart/ Living Etc/ipc Media (Architect: Mooarc); **200 below right** Jean-Francois Jaussaud; **202 left** Alexander Van Verge/VT Wonen/VNU Syndication; **202 right** Richard Powers/Elle Decoration (Architect: Lara Gosling); **203 above & below** Peter Aprahamian; **204 left** Jean-Francois Jaussaud; **204 right** Huntley Headworth/Living Etc/ipc Media; **226** Laurence Monneret/Gettyone Stone

The following photographs have been taken specially for Conran Octopus:

90-95 Thomas Stewart (Architect: Jonathan Pile/Transient); **103** Thomas Stewart (23 Architecture); **114** Thomas Stewart (23 Architecture); **129-131** Thomas Stewart (Theis & Khan Architects); **132-139** Thomas Stewart (Form Design Architecture); **164 right** Thomas Stewart (Architect: Lara Gosling), **187 left & right** Thomas Stewart (Architect: Lara Gosling); **200 left** Thomas Stewart (Architect: Lara Gosling); **201** Thomas Stewart (Architect: Lara Gosling); **205** Thomas Stewart (Architect: Lara Gosling); **207-211** Thomas Stewart (Mark Guard Architects); **213-217** MINH + WASS/Conran Octopus (Roger Hirsch Architect).